Enthusiasm for Midlife Check-In

"This book is a beautifully etched roadmap for midlife. It is infused with great insight, practical wisdom, and valuable tools for the journey."

—TERE LINDSEY, Ph.D., M.A.
Licensed Educational Psychologist
Creator of *Linzey Brain Matters Brain Training Program*

"*Midlife Check-In: Who Am I—Really?* should be required reading for every woman heading into her 40s. From the thoughtful Introduction to the final chapter, MarthaElin's book is filled with nuggets of gold and insightful exercises guaranteed to point you to your True North in midlife and beyond."

—MARY JEANNE VINCENT, M.S.
Career Expert and Strategist
Author of *Career Card Sets: "Acing the Interview," "Beyond the Resume"*
"Career Success Discovery"

"Thoughtful, thorough, gentle and wise, Midlife Check-In offers invaluable guidance and support on the journey to a deepening sense of self."

—SUE PARRIS
Director, Western U.S. Region, NCBI International
Consultant re: Diversity and Inclusion Initiatives,
Leadership Development, Conflict/Dispute Resolution

"You hold in your hands a gem of a book, rich in imagery and content. It reveals the midlife path not by the telling but by direct experience. Dr. Mountain will lead you on your personal and unique path. Enjoy and thrive!"

—STEPHANIE TAYLOR, M.D., Ph.D. (Neurochemistry)
Physician/Healer, A Woman's Wellspring,
Comprehensive Women's Wellness Center

"MarthaElin Mountain offers welcome relief to the futile grasp at perpetual youth by giving us tools to deepen our wells during the prime life phase—midlife. She manages to cover a full spectrum of relevant issues, meeting them with exercises to explore and deepen one's experience. Reading *Midlife Check-In* ignites excitement about this pivotal stage of life. This culture is in dire need of MarthaElin Mountain's voice."

—JENNIFER ALLEN, MFT, ATR-BC
Art Therapist,
Psychotherapist Author of *Bone Knowing: A True Story of*
Coming to Life in the Face of Impending Loss

"I find myself letting go of the old thoughts, beliefs, and habits of doing, but with absolutely no idea of what's on the other side. Before I began reading MarthaElin's book, I didn't even know the questions to ask, other than 'what is wrong with me?' I am so grateful for MarthaElin Mountain and her new book. When I started reading and everything in it resonated with where I am right now, I thought 'Finally! Someone gets it!' I can't wait to share her book, *Midlife Check-In: Who Am I Really?* with all my friends."

—LESLIE BRUHN, CPA, MS Tax
Creator of *Women's Wealth*
Group Program, "*Easiest Record-Keeping System in the World*", and "*Name Your Year*"

"*Midlife Check-In: Who Am I Really?* is a valuable resource for the exploration of the social, emotional, and cognitive challenges and opportunities presented during this developmental phase of life. It has a practical orientation based on interdisciplinary material that guides the reader through the process of self-discovery. *Midlife Check-In* is an ideal book to facilitate this process for individuals, support groups, book groups, as well as clinicians."

—VIRDETTE BRUMM, Ph.D.
Neuropsychologist, Community Hospital
of the Monterey Peninsula, CA.

"Dr. MarthaElin Mountain shares a wealth of wisdom in *Midlife Check-In*. She provides a unique and valuable tool for adults looking to deepen their relationship with their most authentic self. I recommend this book wholeheartedly! She truly supports the reader in a step-by-step process of self-discovery! Thank you, Dr. MarthaElin Mountain!"

—CHRISTINE SANMIQUEL, DTCM, L.Ac., DMQ
Doctor of Traditional Chinese Medicine
Doctor of Medical Qigong, awarded from China

"From MarthaElin Mountain come hundreds of insights that guide you as you experience the journey through midlife. She reveals poignant strategies and provides thought-provoking exercises for women (and men) during this phase of life. If you want to give yourself the gift of clarity, read *Midlife Check-In: Who Am I—Really?*"

—MARION GELLATLY, AICI CIM
President of Powerful Presence
Author of *"Your Powerful Presence . . . 125 Ways to Amplify Your Professional Image;"* Creator of *"Virtual Style School"* and *"Style School LIVE"*

"Midlife Check-In: Who Am I—Really? offers the reader a variety of methods to evaluate the Self. The step-by-step process helps you identify your own needs and experiences while offering a wide range of options for personal expression. The sensitive and gentle approach that Dr. Mountain utilizes allows you to feel safe and nurtured while beginning the journey to determine "who am I *really?*"

—JULIANNE LEAVY, M.A., MFT
Marriage and Family Therapist
Author of *The Innocent Victims*
Founder and Executive Director: *Harmony At Home*
Developer of *Sticks and Stones® Group Counseling Program*

"This *"Check-In"* provides resources for women and men to embrace the expansive horizon of midlife. Brava!"

—TRUDY CORRY RANKIN, Ed.D., LMHC, CST-T,
Psychotherapist, Consultant
Author of *Soul Notes of a Composition:*
In a World Between Two Worlds of Grief from Suicide

"A beautiful guide for people who want to explore their inner world a little deeper. *Midlife Check-In* provides clear and useful guidance and stimulates thoughtful and meaningful introspection. The exercises and questionnaires help the reader evaluate past and present experiences and recognize life purpose and significance. Enjoy!

—GITA MORENA, Ph.D.
Transpersonal Jungian Sandplay Therapist
Author of *The Wisdom of Oz*

"*Midlife Check-In: Who Am I—Really?* is a fresh breath of air. This book is a gift to women going through midlife. I only wish I had had this book available to me when I was experiencing this phase of life."

—DR. MOOJAN DONALDSON, Pharm. D.
Psychopharmacologist
Specialist in Forensic Pharmacy

"As the great Baby Boomer generation reaches Midlife, the question 'Who am I—really?' takes on a more urgent ring. We want to know, we need to know the answer. MarthaElin Mountain's timely, astute, and practical guide helps us to reach deep inside, to the part of ourselves longing to live all of what we were destined to become, to find our timeless essence, the Self. While directed toward those in Midlife, 'Who am I—really?' is a question relevant to all ages."

—LYNNE EHLERS, Ph.D.
Clinical Psychologist in Private Practice
Former Faculty of Dream Studies and
Consciousness Studies, John F. Kennedy University
Author of the forthcoming book *The Alchemical Black,*
White and Red: Stages in the Process of Individuation

Midlife Check-In:
Who Am I—*Really*?

MIDLIFE
☑CHECK-IN:
Who Am I—*Really?*

A Guide to
Deepening Your Sense of Self
In Midlife and Beyond

MarthaElin Mountain
Ed.D., M.A., MFT

authorHOUSE®

AuthorHouse™
1663 Liberty Drive
Bloomington, IN 47403
www.authorhouse.com
Phone: 1-800-839-8640

Published by AuthorHouse 8/31/2012

ISBN: 978-1-4772-5624-4 (sc)
ISBN: 978-1-4772-5623-7 (hc)
ISBN: 978-1-4772-5625-1 (e)

Library of Congress Control Number: 2012914251

This book is not intended as a substitute for consultation or therapy with a trained mental health or medical professional. The author and publisher assume no responsibility for the reader's personal choices in using this book.

Because of the dynamic nature of the Internet, any web addresses or links contained in this book may have changed since publication and may no longer be valid. The views expressed in this work are solely those of the author and do not necessarily reflect the views of the publisher, and the publisher hereby disclaims any responsibility for them.

To
Barbara B. Nelson, M.A., MFT,
who lived the essence of her true Self and,
in so doing, showed many, many of us the way . . .

"Still round the corner
There may wait a new road
Or a secret gate."
J.R. Tolkein

Preface: Your Tree of Midlife

When was the last time you stood in the shelter of a special tree, leaned against one for a quiet moment, or climbed a tree to be held in its embrace? Perhaps it was recently, or perhaps it was long ago? We all need a safe place, from time to time, where we can go and simply "be." We need a personal sanctuary where we can be quiet and reflect—where we can open into ourselves.

This is particularly true for us during our midlife years and beyond. Our need for introspection and developing self-awareness, self-acceptance, and a new perspective is especially great during these years. Your Midlife Check-In process includes a personal sanctuary where you can go for reflection and inspiration.

I believe the familiar tree symbol is an apt metaphor for this personal place. I named it the Tree of Midlife. My hope is that you will come to "know" this tree, or your own version of it, and take shelter there during your Midlife Check-In process.

Upside Down

The tree has been a powerful and meaningful image through the centuries. There is an image of a tree in an eighteenth century Turkish prayer book that is (to our way of seeing things) "upside down." This inverted image is called "Tree of Bliss." It depicts the idea of "growing down" with our roots in the invisible nature beyond us and light years away. The inverted tree, with its roots in heaven, is also found in the Jewish religion as the Qabalistic Tree of Life, and in the tradition of Christian mystics.

When we are born, we normally come into the world headfirst, feet last. In this way, we are inverted. It takes us a lifetime to "get on our feet"—to get to know and connect with the truths of human affairs and Nature's ways, to find our calling and our place with meaning. To plant our feet firmly in the earth with solid "rooting" takes a very long time.

Growing Down

We seem always to be growing down. We leave our protected home base to enter a wider world, whether for school, work, or new relationships. Each heartbreak and rejection grows us down. Experiences in darker and, sometimes, despairing places in our life grow us down. They deepen our roots into the life force within the earth and our self. We also grow down when we take quiet time to rest and reflect—to lean against our tree.

A New Energy in You

Nature intends for us to grow down in our midlife years and beyond so that we can become more of who we are meant to be. This developmental process is built into us. You have left the years of childhood, adolescence, and young adulthood when you were psychologically grafted onto and sustained by a parent's roots. You have moved through the initial years of adulthood, when you began to strike root yourself in the ground of personal transformation.

A new energy is emerging within you now. Its intention is a kind of sacred unfolding, as a tree unfolds into its fullness of maturity. The unfolding is inward, toward your depths and away from the outer world. The transformative powers of Nature are at work in you.

A Powerful Image

The tree is a powerful image of what nature intends our midlife and later years to be about: an intense inner life connecting us with the hidden and deeper place of who we are *really*. The tree has come into existence from a tiny bare seed of potential with built-in aspirations for growth. It represents the "evergreen" within each of us.

Your Tree of Midlife is a wise and powerful ally. Its connection between above and below is firm, its physical presence is useful and beautiful. It *knows* who it is and it lives who it is naturally. Your tree supports you in your process of growth and transformation. Its roots provide a strong and stable foundation. Your tree's roots push downward for nourishment, embracing the layers of your triumphs, skills, and lessons learned. They embrace the layers of your fears, defenses, regrets, and resentments. They thrive in the depths and instincts of who you are at your core.

A Safe Place

The sheltering branches of your midlife tree will offer a safe place to be during your Midlife Check-In process. Becoming comfortable there will be important. Climb the sturdy trunk, the bridge between roots and branches. Trust its strength and adjoining branches to support your feet and body as you go. Find a favorite place in your tree and let the branches hold and steady you, with balance and resilience.

A Mentor

Your tree is a mentor, of sorts, for your process of personal growth and transformation. It inspires by example, meeting each season and holding its ground, whether blooming or bare. The life force at its core nudges it continuously to grow into its fullest. Its roots deepen in places unseen and grow down into wisdom, while branches and new growth reach for the light.

A Witness

Your Tree of Midlife is a presence and a witness to life. Birds have perched in it to sing and give warning. They have built nests, laid eggs, and hatched life in your tree. Various creatures have crawled and scurried on its trunk and through the branches. They have nestled in the safety of your tree. Young birds have taken first flights from these branches. Treasures have been hidden in your tree's hollowed out places, and lives have suffered beneath its branches. The sun has warmed your midlife tree—and the sky has wept upon it.

Under the Moon and Stars

Being in your Tree of Midlife in the darkness, with just the moon and the stars as your guests, can be very valuable at times. Something deeper and wiser often stirs in us in our darkest hours; growth begins there. Our deepest and truest Self (some call it "soul") awakens in the darkness.

Make It Your Own

The Tree of Midlife will be just another tree until it takes on meaning for you at a deeper and more personal level. Your Midlife Check-In process will help you make this connection. You will have opportunities to climb down from your tree and change your vantage point. You will sit under it or lean against it and reflect.

Make this tree your own. You may alter it in some ways. For example, you may decide to remove some of its branches. You may want to add signs of life experiences, such as knotholes, broken limbs, or additional fallen leaves. While you are at it, why not carve a heart or two in its trunk? Or hang a sign on it? If you would like birds or other creatures to join you in your personal sanctuary, invite them into your tree. The Tree of Midlife is yours. Imagine this sanctuary for yourself. Turn it upside-down, if you like, as others before you have done.

Your Midlife Tree Is Wise

Your tree is wise. It *knows* who it is and it *lives* who it is naturally. Your tree also speaks to you. Pause. Listen gently with your soul ear. Your midlife tree may speak in the rustling of its leaves as the wind passes through, in the creaking of its limbs, or as branches meet and touch one another. Your tree may speak without any sounds at all. You will come to "know" its voice. Let it speak through you of possibilities not yet considered and of new and different ways of thinking.

Feel Held

Let your Tree of Midlife embrace you. Feel held in the spaces between its branches. Let your tree strengthen you. Be as you are in the moment—and lose track of time.

This personal sanctuary is a cradle for ideas, insights, and images that want to emerge and grow in you. Inspiration lives in this nurturing place. I know this well—it was in the soulful embrace of my own midlife tree that I was inspired to write this book.

ꝑ

Oh, and by the way . . . your Tree of Midlife may *look* similar to other trees, but it is unique. There is a door in it that opens inward . . .

MarthaElin Mountain
Midlife Check-In, 2012

Table of Contents

ȸ

List of Illustrations

Introduction

This book is a celebration of the simple, yet enduring fact that you are far more than you may believe. "Who" you are is—all at once—who you have been, who you are now, and who you are *really*. All of this is "you." And, no matter where you are in midlife or beyond, possibilities for becoming more than you have before await you! The part of you who is wise already knows what those possibilities are. Your Midlife Check-In process will help you to discover them.

1. Lines and Spaces
2. The Three Urgent Questions
3. The Four Parts of This Book
4. Special Features
5. Sources
6. Men and Women Midlife Travelers
7. Ways to Use This Book
8. The Midlife Check-In Process
9. Brain-Body-Mind-Spirit
10. *Your* Process

1. Lines and Spaces

Lines: When I was in my early twenties, feeling all "grown up," I believed that my life would follow a straight line: I would build my career, meet my life partner, and live a predictable set of rhythms until I grew "old." I actually believed that, while things around me might change, I would stay the same. I just had to stay on that straight line.

The straight line I thought I would follow through life had been drawn mostly by others. I worked hard to stay on it. How well I could stay on the line was my measure of success. To stray off of the line could mean society's disapproval.

What staying on the line really meant, however, and what I could not have known at the time, was that, by working hard to conform and stay on the line, I was constraining myself. I was relinquishing my uniqueness and my chances for becoming whole; I was trading in who I was *really* for the safety of meeting others' expectations. Somehow, I did not consider drawing some of my *own* lines!

As time went on, I began noticing it was not so easy—or fulfilling— to live my life entirely on the line. Something was nudging me from inside to stray off of the line and to draw my own lines. Fortunately for me, as I moved into increasingly responsible positions, I encountered mentors, new friends, and gifted leaders. I noticed how they made a difference by drawing their own lines and, at times, stepping into the spaces *between* the lines. Could I do that?

Spaces: Inspired by these examples, I began to risk stepping off of the line and into the spaces, little by little. I played with my imagination and creative energies in new ways, valued times for reflection, engaged in more fulfilling relationships, and encountered fertile ideas waiting to be nurtured. I initiated innovative projects and professional programs. I was beginning to express my more authentic Self.

Then, one day, I left the professional life I had known and loved for so many years to chart a new course for myself. I felt free; my life seemed to be taking on new meaning.

Looking back, I can see that meeting certain requirements, on the line, did pay off over the years. I gained access to opportunities I might not have had otherwise. Had I kept trying to live *all* of my life on the line, however, I would have closed myself off from my true Self. And, by contrast, had I decided to live all of my life in the spaces, I would have closed myself off from the world.

I see now that the lines connect our day-to-day events and experiences. They connect us to others and to the outside world through shared norms, respect, and beliefs. Lines are important in this respect.

The spaces—in between the lines and under the surface of things—contain more than what we see or hear. They contain the gifts of lessons learned, insights acquired, and inspirations about who we have been, who we are now, and who we are meant to become. They contain possibilities of things not yet imagined.

Spaces hold those feelings and intuitions which daily life does not have a place for and mostly seems to suppress. In the spaces, there is a meandering of soul—of compassion, empathy, creativity, and vulnerability. While the lines seem to matter more to us in our earlier years, it is the spaces *between* the lines that are calling to us in midlife and beyond.

What I could not understand in my early twenties and have come to realize, over time, is that my life and I, along with the lines and spaces, are forever changing—both outside and inside. Growth will continue throughout my life; it did not end at "adulthood." Some lines I followed in my past have become entangled with the new lines I am drawing now. Some lines have separated and gone their own ways, and some have doubled back. Other lines were detours or dead ends. Where I have gone in circles, searching for meaning, and where I have encountered the same lessons to be learned, time and again, the lines spiral. They reveal my ongoing pilgrimage around (and around!) my center, or true Self, sometimes moving inward and closer, and other times shifting outward and away.

Travelling the spiral lines, lines that double back, and new lines that I draw is a way of seeking answers to the urgent and deeper questions in my life. Stepping into spaces *between* the lines helps me grow *into* those questions.

2. The Three Urgent Questions

Who have I been? Who am I now? Who am I *really*? You and the three urgent question in Part Three are travelling companions. They live in the spaces between your lifelines. These questions work in, on, and with you—especially through your middle years and beyond. Although I have sequenced the questions for a kind of chronological exploration, they do not swim around in us sequentially. They ebb and flow in us, as *we* do in *them*.

The three questions matter. The relationship you develop with them in midlife has a direct affect on how you will live your life in later years. In order to take charge of the direction and authenticity of who you become, you must engage with these questions. To ask each one and give honest answers requires a certain amount of courage and self-trust. To become more authentic you will have to lean into the questions closely and put your ear to the deeper and wiser part of yourself. Exploring the three questions in this way sharpens your eye on the journey. Midlife Check-In is designed to help you do this.

3. The Four Parts of This Book

The information in Midlife Check-In is arranged as a progressive, interactive process for opening to your authentic nature. The prompts, exercises, and self-assessments will expose you, gradually, to deeper levels of your inner experience. Midlife Check-In has four parts:

Part One: Getting Ready for Your Midlife Check-In
Part Two: The Three Phases of Midlife
Part Three: The Three Urgent Questions of Midlife
Part Four: Now What? Who and How Am I Becoming?

Part One: Getting Ready for Your Midlife Check-In: The two chapters in Part One will prepare you for your check-in process. Chapter One, "Tools and Personal Choices," will help you make the process your own. Chapter Two, "What Am I Feeling?" will give you a heads-up about feelings, how yours may emerge in the process, and ways to manage them in healthy ways.

Part Two: The Three Phases of Midlife: Part Two has five chapters. Chapter Three is "The Midlife Checklist©" which, over time, went through several iterations, as I field-tested it for accuracy and clarity. This instrument is based on extensive research about midlife shifts and challenges and on my professional and personal observations. This unique self-assessment instrument gives you two important kinds of information about yourself:

1. Which psychological phase(s) of midlife you are in now, and
2. Which of life's Seven Threads of Becoming are the most prominent in your life at this time.

The Midlife Checklist© consists of fifty statements that represent inner and outer experiences of women and men in midlife. No one experiences all of these. Certain ones, however, are more typical of one phase in midlife than of the other two. *(And, by the way, if you want to find out what emotional experiences and behaviors are considered normal or not in midlife, you will find answers in Appendix A: What's Normal? What's Not?)*

Chapter Four, "My Midlife Checklist© Results: What Do They Mean?" explains your results and clarifies their meaning. Chapter Five, "The Three Phases of Midlife: Moons, Meanings, Murmurings, Movement" provides a detailed description of each of the midlife phases and the symbolism of the moon in relation to each of them. Chapter Six, "Midlife and the Seven Threads of Becoming: How They Weave Their Colors into Midlife," describes the Seven Threads with specific examples of their presence in midlife. You may recognize a few of them. Chapter Seven, "But Wait! What About the *Full* Moon?" addresses an interesting question for you to consider.

Part Three: The Three Urgent Questions of Midlife: Part Three is the heart of your Midlife Check-In process. It has three chapters, each devoted to one of the three core questions that swim around in us, especially during our midlife years: Who have I been? Who am I now? Who am I *really*? Each chapter includes self-assessments, exercises, and explanations related to the chapter's focus question. In each case, they are designed to increase and deepen your self-knowledge, -awareness, and -understanding. Your work in Part Three is essential; it will prepare you for your next steps in Part Four.

Part Four: Now What? Who and How Am I Becoming? There are two chapters in Part Four. Chapter Eleven focuses your attention on "Five Brief Exercises," designed and sequenced to help you capture what lies at the heart of your authentic nature. In Chapter Twelve, you will create a template of the qualities, image, and voice of the more authentic person you imagine becoming. This template will be credible, meaningful, and inspiring to you because it will be grounded in self-knowledge,—understanding, and—awareness you acquired in your Midlife Check-In process.

4. Special Features

There is a variety of special features in your Midlife Check-In book. In addition to Appendix A "What's Normal? What's Not?, the Midlife Glossary, an extensive Bibliography and film list, and a detailed Index, there are three special features I would like to highlight:

- Checklist Format
- Back Pocket
- Therapist's Practical Guide

Checklist Format: I have used the checklist format for many of the exercises and prompts in Midlife Check-In. A checklist is an efficient way to help you identify the factors most relevant to you in a series of choices.

Checklists act as a cognitive safety net. That is, they catch examples and ideas that you might otherwise not have considered to be important in your experience. They capture information you may not have thought about for a long time—they jog your memory. Checklists can also bring your attention to the things you may be tempted to discard.

The exercises and self-assessments in Midlife Check-In are not about right-or-wrong answers. They are about honest responses. Let the questions and the information invoke in you a deeper level of experience with a sense of what is true for you. Allow them to give you a sense of direction for becoming more authentic.

Back Pocket: As you work through your check-in process, you may want to note ideas and insights, questions that occur to you, results of self-assessments, and other information with special meaning. At the very end of the book, after the Index, you will find the Back Pocket that is designed just for this purpose. Back Pocket is a "container" for information you want to keep track of and refer to later—like having a notebook you can tuck into your jacket, purse, or back pocket! At various points in your check-in process, you will be prompted to write your ideas or observations in your Back Pocket (or a personal notebook, if you prefer). Mark this section with a sticky note or turn down the corner. This will help you find it easily when you need it.

Therapist's Practical Guide: This Guide speaks directly to clinicians and gives specific ideas for using the book with individuals and groups. It includes a handy cross-referenced list of all exercises and their specific purpose. It also includes lists of suggested Midlife Check-In materials for the initial phase of therapy, for tracking client progress, for educating clients, for deepening the work, and for life review. Most of the exercises in this book are appropriate for use with women and men in their midlife years and beyond.

5. Sources

I researched material for this book from a range of scholarly and other resources in a variety of disciplines, including: Sociology, Movement and Dance, Science and Neurophysiology, Literature of poetry and prose, Education, and Jungian psychology. In my writing process, I drew from this interdisciplinary material and, in large measure, from the well of my experience as a therapist and educator, midlife traveler, and group leader for elders and midlife women.

An unusual and interesting source of information for this book are the "full-moon women" in their 70s, 80s, and 90s who agreed to participate in my book with information about their own midlife experiences and turning points. They have lived their midlife years and can look back on them with a meaningful perspective. These women also offered advice for women who are currently in their middle years. I have quoted them at the end of Chapter Five and on the title page for each part of this book.

6. Men and Women Midlife Travelers

Midlife Check-In is a self-discovery process that is appropriate for both women and men. While a part of the book, here or there, may reflect a more feminine focus, the majority of Midlife Check-In will resonate for both genders.

There are clear differences between some of the ways men and women experience their midlife years. The felt urgency to address shifts and issues is generally greater for women than it is for men, and the nature of some inner shifts is different for both. Men's propensity for talking about personal midlife experiences, or for seeking professional support, is typically expressed later, rather than sooner, if at all. That being said, however, the requirements for growing into one's wholeness or true Self remain the same for us all.

The Midlife Checklist©, with the exception of the last seven items, reflects common experiences of male and female midlife travelers. I have included seven separate items for women and for men at the end of the Checklist to accommodate certain known differences.

7. Ways To Use This Book

Midlife Check-In can be used by individuals and by groups.

Individuals: Here are four ways an individual may want to use this book:

1. Engage in the full self-help process, Parts One through Four
2. Use it as a handy resource for facts and other information about midlife
3. Complete the Midlife Checklist© to understand what phase(s) of midlife one is in and which of the Seven Threads of Becoming are prominent in one's life at this time.
4. Use it as an adjunct to a personal therapy process

Support Group: This book is an excellent resource for a group of six to ten people focused on midlife experiences and their meanings. Ideally, the group would be led by a skilled professional with experience in group facilitation and with expertise in the facts and concerns related to the midlife years. It is essential for all group members to have a strong sense of trust among themselves and to feel that the setting where they meet is a safe space for sharing confidences. *This is extremely important.*

Book Group: A book group may choose Midlife Check-In as their focus for discussion. Part Two offers self-assessments, as well as factual information about the midlife phases, personal issues, and experiences. Group discussions might focus on the information in Part Two and the Appendices, while individuals move through Parts Three and Four on their own. If a book group is reading another book related to midlife, Midlife Check-In is an excellent companion to use as a reference and for assessing personal midlife experiences.

8. The Midlife Check-In Process

The Midlife Check-In process is structured "just enough" to be a safe container for inner work, without restricting you to "staying on the lines." It will move you, in fact, into the spaces *between* the lines and help you connect with your more authentic Self.

In order to maintain a practical orientation and to keep the focus on your process, I have introduced important concepts and facts at a basic level. My intent has been to incorporate them in ways that honor your need as a reader for clear and helpful explanations with practical value. Some of the central concepts include: Self, wholeness, integration, authenticity, consciousness, unconscious, emotional wounding, identity, and psyche.

The Midlife Check-In process is a blend of the factual, experiential, and imaginal realms. It is a progressive, interactive process of deepening Self-discovery, one that is intimate and empowering. As you work with your Check-In process, you will recall, notice, reflect, and act. You will experience, observe, learn, and wonder. You will imagine, explore, decide, and create.

I have folded education and whimsy into this Self-discovery process. In some ways, your experiences in the process will pique your curiosity and be fun; in others they will be deeply moving. The Midlife Check-In process will affirm you and your quest for Self-meaning. I hope it will enlighten you, as well. It is definitely an opportunity for you to be with your midlife experience and not run away.

While I cannot be physically present to witness your process and engage with you personally, my intention has been to create an atmosphere of safety and encouragement for you in the Midlife Check-In process.

✍**NOTE**: You will notice that in some places of the book I spell s-e-l-f with a lower case "s" and in other places I use a capital "S." I use the first one to mean the ego or personality, the conscious part of us. I use the second one to means *all* of our psychological and soulful processes, both conscious and unconscious. Chapter Ten will clarify the differences in more detail.

9. Brain-Body-Mind-Spirit

This book wants to build your awareness of how the Check-In process may speak to you through body sensations, mind activity, and spirit or "inner knowing." The dynamics of body, mind, and spirit are continuously alive in us and speaking to us, whether we are conscious of them or not. Through Midlife Check-In I will encourage you to pause and take notice of body tension, feelings, and unexpected insights. I will encourage you to find meaningful ways to express them.

There is an important reason for doing so: As you awaken dormant places and bring inner expression alive in you, you gradually free yourself to let imagination do its work and connect you with who you are—*really*.

10. *Your* Process

There is no "right" way to engage in your Midlife Check-In process. You may want to skim the book first for content and an overview of the process, and then go back and begin. You might begin with Part One and continue through Part Four. You may read and work, pausing for a time between the parts. You might choose to allow more time in your process for reflection and artistic expression of feelings that emerge in you. Be flexible with yourself as you engage in your process. Follow your own path and rhythms. Trust your instincts, and follow where they lead you.

At different times, the material will resonate for you in heart, mind, and soul. Sometimes it will not. Trust that you will draw from your Check-In process what you need in the moment.

I want you to notice how what you are focused on affects your body and how you are feeling. Perhaps something has hit a sensitive place in you and stirred a deeper response. Take breaks. Climb down from your midlife tree and lean against it. Relax. Reflect. I have written more about this in Part One.

Midlife Check-In intends to deepen your sense of Self by nudging you into the spaces between your lines. It will ask you to meet yourself head-on, answer some tough questions, and take conscious steps toward becoming the more authentic person you are meant to be. It will awaken in you what might have fallen asleep.

Be patient with yourself. Becoming who you are meant to be is a gradual, naturally unfolding of Self; it is not about instant change. This journey toward wholeness and true Self is—at once—universal in the span of the life process *and* uniquely yours, distinct from any other.

As your Self-awareness increases and your connection with who you really are deepens, the possibilities for living more authentically will stir in you, take root, and grow. A wise place in you already knows what those possibilities are; Midlife Check-In will help you discover them.

Stay open. Trust the process, and go at your own pace. Now, open the door inward, and begin . . .

MarthaElin Mountain
2012

ONE

Getting Ready for Your Midlife Check-In

&

Chapter One
Tools and Personal Choices

Chapter Two
What Am I Feeling?

> *"Ask yourself if your current lifestyle is working for you and is what you want to continue. If not, then dare to take the risk to move on."*
> Barbara, Full-Moon Woman, age 81

Chapter One

Tools and Personal Choices

Midlife Check-In is a personal journey—one you can settle into. We "settle into" something when we feel safe and comfortable. Picture a place you have known that felt safe, comfortable, and relaxed for you. Maybe it was a particular room or space in a room, a place in nature, or someone's home. When you were a child, it may have been someone's lap.

Think about that special place. Feel how you have settled into it before. Enjoy the memory as you begin to settle into your Midlife Check-In process.

I encourage you to find a physical space that feels safe and comfortable for engaging in your process. Make it your own with some of the suggestions in this chapter. Make it a place you will look forward to settling into.

Two Sections: Tools and Personal Choices

The two sections below, "Tools" and "Personal Choices," will help you settle into your Midlife Check-In process. The first section suggests some tools you may want to have handy.

The second section includes choices for personalizing your check-in process. By considering your preferences in advance, you are taking charge of your journey and beginning to settle in.

TOOLS

There are four kinds of tools to consider. These include tools for:
- Comfort and Safety
- Self-Awareness
- Self-Expression
- Keeping Track of My Thoughts, Insights, and Questions

Just as your Midlife Check-In experience will be unique, so will the combination of your tools. Which ones appeal to *you*? Which ones would work easily with your usual style? Put a check by the tools in each category that you feel drawn to at this time.

Remember to turn off phone, pager, or anything else that beeps.

Comfort and Safety
__Quiet, private environment that calms me
__Calming music
__Singing bowl, chime, or bell with a soothing tone
__Inspiring photo of myself or of someone I admire deeply
__A cozy blanket or shawl to wrap up in as I read and reflect
__A splash of cold water on my face
__Periodic breaks: Take a walk, even just to another part of my home; step into nature; prepare a sit-down healthy lunch for myself and take time to savor each bite

Self-Awareness
__Mind open to possibilities
__My observer self who can stand alongside of me as a personal witness
__Empathy and compassion for myself
__"The Feelings Gauge" (page 8) for checking in with my feelings
__Trust in that part of me that is wise and gives good counsel

<u>**Self-Expression**</u> (See end of chapter for *A Note About Self-Expression* and *A Note About Movement* page 5.)

__Music to help me express feelings (such as joy, inner peace, sadness, excitement) through movement, art, voice

__Airy scarves that float when I move with them

__Art materials: scissors, glue, crayons, colored pencils, colored pens/markers/construction paper, clay, paints, digital programs

Keeping Track of My Thoughts, Insights and Questions

—My favorite pen or pencil

—Highlighter(s)

__"Back Pocket" (at the end of the book): A place to jot notes, keep track of your insights, ideas, and questions as you go through the process

__A blank personal notebook

(An unlined journal gives you more freedom. Instead of jotting down words, your writing tool may want to draw something or scribble unexpectedly!)

PERSONAL CHOICES

<u>Consider the following questions and your personal preferences for:</u>

- Comfort and Safety
  - Self-Awareness
  - Self-Expression
- Keeping Track of My Thoughts, Insights, and Questions

Comfort and Safety

- What physical space(s) will be the most comfortable for me while I am "checking in?"

- Who might I look to for inspiration, sharing, or emotional support?

Self-Awareness

- When is the best time for me to "check in?" (Daily? One day a week? On the weekend? Early a.m.? During p.m.? Randomly? On a personal retreat?)

Self-Expression (See end of chapter for *A Note About Self-Expression* and *A Note About Movement*, page 5.)

- Which of the following ways might I use to express my feelings and thoughts?

 ___writing
 ___sculpting with clay
 ___painting
 ___using my voice in nature
 ___sketching
 ___sharing w/a trusted friend
 ___drawing
 ___photos or other images
 ___creative movement
 ___collaging
 ___graphic arts

Keeping Track of My Thoughts, Insights, and Questions

- Will I record my thoughts, insights, and questions in the Back Pocket or in my personal notebook?

- Where will I keep my Midlife Check-In book and notes?

✍ A Note About Self-Expression

If journaling, art, music, movement, or quiet-time practice is not a part of your life, consider which one or ones might be interesting for you to explore. Remember: There is not a "right" way to use any of the techniques or media; they are for individual expression. They can allow different parts of you to "speak" about who you are and how you are. What these parts will share, when you give them freedom to express, may surprise and relieve you! Expressing yourself through the arts can gradually free you to let your imagination connect you with the spaces between the lines.

✍ A Note About Movement

(This is not about dancing ability; it is about your willingness to move in a safe space.)

"Self-movement," or authentic movement, is "a naturally learned expression of man" (Diem (1970) in Chaitlin). Trying out movements smaller and larger, slower and faster, you can actually feel new confidence in being.

By allowing your body to move freely and with increasing spontaneity, you can feel a confidence in yourself as a worthwhile and esteemed human being. Activating your muscles and joints and making physical contact with the floor or ground can help you be in closer touch with yourself within the space; you live the experience in the moment!

Your personal movement repertoire is acquired over time through sensing and feeling, and by trying, experimenting, and creating. Moving your body and exploring the here-and-now in a defined space can help you "test" your sense of self.

When you are expressing yourself with authentic, free movements that are prompted from within you, you are moving toward greater self-expression, increased self-control, better self-understanding, increasing self-responsibility, more independence, and greater self-realization in becoming a whole person. (Ideas adapted from Chaitlin, page 87.)

Chapter Two

What Am I Feeling?

Midlife affects our feelings in new and, sometimes, strange ways. As you work with the exercises in Midlife Check-In, feelings may come up, from an unexpected chuckle to tension or tears. I recommend that you stop, every so often, notice your body state, and check in with how you are feeling. The "Feelings Gauge" described on page 8, will help you do this.

Truth Tellers

Your feelings and body sensations are your brain's messengers; they let you know the true state of your body, mind, and spirit. They are truth-tellers. We often fool ourselves about how we are feeling. For example, my thoughts and beliefs may be telling me one thing *("I'm fine!")*, while my feelings and body sensations are telling a different story *("This is uncomfortable." "I don't want to think about this." "I feel ashamed when that thought/memory enters my mind." "I'm anxious." "I feel sad.")*. Our clenched jaw, furrowed brow, tight stomach, locked knees, or headache tells us the truth.

On the other hand, my thoughts and beliefs may be telling me, *"All is well. I am at peace with this,"* and my body reveals that I truly am. My breathing is calm, my shoulders are relaxed and open, I feel centered, and my heart is beating at a comfortable rate.

Lying

We want to maintain harmony with others or avoid conflict, and so we tell lies. We say things like: "I'm fine" or "Everything's good." When we deny or repress the truth of our feelings, we tell lies at the emotional or body level; we lose our integrity. When we do this, there is a tension inside of us and our body, and a body part may show it. For example, our hands may clench each other, our shoulders may sag forward, our eyes may widen, our knees may lock, or our mouth may suggest sadness. Over time, being out of touch with our self emotionally can translate into physical symptoms or functional change.

The truth is not always easy for us to recognize. We may have to work to discover it. When we are in touch with what we really feel, we are better able to face our pain. When we connect with our pain and acknowledge it, we are true to ourselves.

How We Avoid Feeling Our Feelings

Some individuals live such intense lives that they do not have time for their feelings. They live life primarily from their left brain, the Land of Reason, where rational and analytical thinking rule. They are focused on what is happening from their neck up!

Many of us learned, early on, to be *afraid* of the feelings inside of ourselves. Through first-hand experiences and observations of our family's behaviors, we learned that expressing feelings was not ok or not safe; our true feelings were simply not acceptable. So, over the years, we played it safe and faked it. We separated from our feelings, and we buried our truth.

The fear of expressing true feelings can lead us to block out or "forget" certain unhappy or painful experiences. When we do this, we disconnect from our authentic Self, from who we are really.

Connect and Grow

When we *do* acknowledge our feelings and learn healthy ways to manage and express them, we become more authentic. We enhance our emotional, physical and spiritual well-being. *And* we grow.

WHAT ARE YOU FEELING—*IN THIS MOMENT?*

Pause, now. Notice the sensations or "messages" your body is giving to you *in this moment.* Do a quick body scan: Begin at the top of your head. Notice your scalp, eyes, and jaw area. Is there tightness anywhere? Notice your shoulders: Are they pulled forward, or are they relaxed and down? Scan your torso, each arm and hand, and both legs and feet. Is there tension anywhere?

If you notice any tension or discomfort, such as tightness, pain, or churning, where is it in your body? Be sure to notice, also, which part of your body is most relaxed. Just notice . . . and breathe.

Use the Feelings Gauge below to help you zero in on your feelings *in this moment. Then explore "21 Ways I Can take Care of Myself Right Now" and identify ways to calm yourself, as needed.*

FEELINGS GAUGE:
WHAT AM I FEELING, *RIGHT NOW?* ©

Circle the number on the scale below that best describes how you are feeling *right now, in this very moment.* **0** represents the calmest feeling state and **10** represents the most upset feeling state. Descriptions of associated body sensations are shown at each extreme to help you gauge where your feelings are *in this moment.*

0 . . .1 . . .2 . . .3 . . .4 . . .5 . . .6 . . .7 . . .8 . . .9 . . .10

Clear	Confused
Centered	Scattered
Relaxed, Still	Tense, Agitated
Nonjudgmental	Reactive, Critical
Slow deep breathing	Rapid breathing
Resting pulse rate	Fast pulse
In total peace	On high alert

Using the Feelings Gauge, which you will find in nearly every chapter, will help you to practice inner tracking of your current emotional state and deepen your mind-body-spirit connection.

21 WAYS I CAN TAKE CARE OF MYSELF
RIGHT NOW

It is important to have simple and effective ways to manage your tension and uncomfortable feelings in the moment. Below are 21 ideas. Using these can help you move quickly toward a more relaxed and balanced state of being.

☑ Check the ones you like most:

☐ Breathe deeply and slowly

☐ Move freely to music

☐ Stand, stretch, walk around

☐ Do 10-20 jumping jacks

☐ then forward slightly such as Bend gently side to side,

☐ Beat a drum

☐ Light a candle and be with its light for a few minutes

☐ Hold or stroke my pet

☐ Move to a different space

☐ Watch a funny movie

☐ Climb into my midlife tree

☐ Be in nature near flowers, trees, water, soothing views

☐ Hug myself and breathe

☐ Ring my singing bowl

☐ Speak with a trusted friend

☐ Drink a warm beverage herbal tea, milk, soup

☐ Laugh out loud

☐ Shift my body position and breathe deeply

☐ Place my hands over my heart

☐ Focus on an inspiring image

☐ Make a positive statement about myself

℘ **NOTE:** If you happen to experience feelings of distress it may be time to take a break and relax. Symptoms may include: tension building in your chest, throat tightening, jaw clenching, tears, breathing on hold, nausea, urge to scream or yell, headache. If painful feelings are hard for you to manage in healthful ways, consider seeking professional help.

TWO

The Three Phases of Midlife

&
ɓ

Introduction

Chapter Three
The Midlife Checklist©:
Which Phase or Phases of Midlife Am I In?

Chapter Four
My Midlife Checklist© Results:
What Do They Mean?

Chapter Five
The Three Midlife Phases:
Their Moons, Meanings, Murmurings, Movement

Chapter Six
Midlife and the Seven Threads of Becoming:
How Do They Weave Themselves into Our Midlife Years?

Chapter Seven
But Wait! What About the *Full* Moon?

> *"My most valuable midlife experience was my struggle to learn how to relate lovingly, trust others, and stay present and centered."*
>
> Barbara, Full-Moon Woman, 90

Introduction

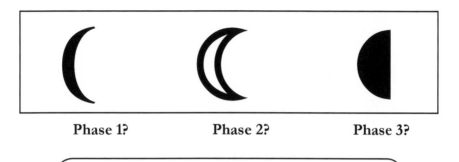

Phase 1? **Phase 2?** **Phase 3?**

"Who looks outside, dreams. Who looks inside, awakens."
Carl Gustav Jung

In Chapter Three, you will identify two kinds of information about yourself: 1) the psychological phase(s) of midlife you are in, and 2) which of the Seven Threads of Becoming are weaving themselves most prominently into your life at this time. Your results of the Midlife Checklist© will give you this information.

The Midlife Checklist© focuses your attention on fifty inner experiences and outer behaviors that are typical for women and men at various times in their midlife transition. It asks you to ☑ the items that *feel true* for you at this time or *have felt true* for you during the last six months. The Midlife Checklist© is a kind of "GPS" for locating your current position(s) on the spectrum of the middle years.

Chapter Four shows you the meanings of your choices on the Midlife Checklist©. Chapter Five gives detailed descriptions of the three phases of midlife, how they ebb and flow in us, and the many gifts inherent in them. Chapter Six provides specific examples of the sorts of things that can come up in midlife in relation to the Seven Threads of Becoming that weave themselves in and out of our life. These threads include: **A**uthenticity, **B**ody, **C**reative Energy, **H**eart

Matters, Identity, Loss and Grief, and Relationship. Chapter Seven raises and answers an important question.

The Midlife Checklist© has no "right" answers. Choose *your* answers by listening closely to what you know to be true for you, based on your experience. Take note of what *feels* true and let these honest feelings guide your answers. After completing The Midlife Checklist©, follow the accompanying directions in "How to Find and Record Your Results."

It is time to turn the page and begin. Are you and your pencil ready?

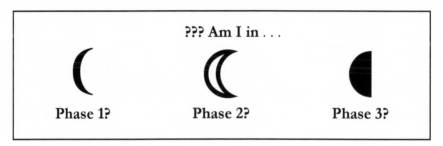

??? Am I in . . .

Phase 1?   Phase 2?   Phase 3?

**Which of the Seven Threads of Becoming
are weaving themselves into my life now?**
A?   B?   C?   H?   I?   L?   R?

Chapter Three

The Midlife Checklist©
MarthaElin Mountain, Ed.D., M.A., MFT

DIRECTIONS

The following ☑-list focuses on typical midlife experiences and behaviors. There are 50 items. Read each one and ask yourself: "Does this statement <u>feel true</u> about my personal experience *within the last six months?*" Notice if the statement resonates for you—if it *feels* or has felt familiar to you, during the past six months. If it does, check ☑ it. There can be no "right" or "wrong" answers to the Midlife Checklist©. Your responses will vary from anyone else's because of the unique aspects and experiences of who you are. Simply ☑ what is true for *you*. Items #44-50 are in two sets: one for women and one for men.

☐ 1. I want to keep the lifestyle of my 20s and early 30s alive.

☐ 2. Regrets or dissatisfactions about my life are creeping in.

☐ 3. I question my sensual and sexual appeal. I feel vulnerable in sexual or other intimate relationships.

☐ 4. More often than not, I feel a clear inner calm about where I am headed.

☐ 5. I am more and more selective about how I spend my time; I am less inclined to "do it all."

☐ 6. "Newness" draws me: new physical appearance, new pursuits, new partner(s).

☐ 7. Earlier dreams of happiness are melting away or have been shattered abruptly.

☐ 8. Something *deeper* than work, job, or career is calling to me.

☐ 9. I have a sense that there *is* light at the end of the tunnel.

☐ 10. People I used to idealize now disappointment me; new feelings of self-doubt and of doubt about my relationships are coming up.

☐ 11. I am losing older loved ones more often.

☐ 12. I have a strong sense of wanting to leave something of myself to the world.

☐ 13. Sometimes I have the urge to abandon the life I have for something entirely different.

☐ 14. I change jobs or relationships in hopes of changing my sense of who I am.

☐ 15. I am becoming less focused on the "cracks" in my physical image and more focused on who I am on the inside.

☐ 16. I feel a deep sense of being part of a larger web of influences in the world.

☐ 17. The script of past years that told me what to do next in life no longer fits.

☐ 18. I have a sense of hanging in suspension, as if my past is being amputated.

☐ 19. Life is generally less exciting, even boring.

☐ 20. There are parts of me that I keep hidden—parts that can be a bit villainous or mean-spirited at times.

☐ 21. More and more, I limit my relationships to ones I truly enjoy or want to nurture.

☐ 22. I am very comfortable with who I am; I am more flexible with gender roles and not concerned with traditional views of my role.

☐ 23. I feel I'm being prepared for something that is not clear, yet; there is a kind of "undressing" going on.

☐ 24. While I used to find it hard to accept, I *get* it, now: death is a fact of my life.

☐ 25. I am letting go of things I acquired over the years that I don't need or want anymore.

☐ 26. It feels as if there is an "unlived life" hiding within me waiting to be lived.

☐ 27. I find that my parents, or others in their generation, are increasingly dependent on me for support in one form or another. Our roles seem to be reversing.

☐ 28. I feel cast adrift now that my children have left home.

☐ 29. An earlier feeling of having "arrived" in life seems less grounded.

☐ 30. My main goals, at this time, are for positive outcomes for me and my career, and/or for my growing family.

☐ 31. I am asking, "Whose life have I been living? Whose values have directed my choices?"

☐ 32. My earlier self-image is cracking and altering; physical signs of aging are beginning to show.

☐ 33. I have become curious about life in ways I wasn't before. Sometimes I feel like a curious little kid!

☐ 34. Something is missing in my primary relationships. I ask myself, "What have I neglected? What should I change?" There are intimate feelings longing to be expressed and I feel stuck, not clear about what to do with them.

☐ 35. There are several things I want to acquire in order to build a comfort-able life for the long term.

☐ 36. I often feel I am just going through empty motions. I have lost interest in things and feel apathetic.

☐ 37. Increasingly, I am able to love others and enjoy intimacy without any hidden agendas.

☐ 38. A certain fear about my future (and the future of my nuclear family) creeps in from time to time.

☐ 39. I ask myself *often*, "What does my soul want of me?"

☐ 40. It feels as if I'm approaching a door that is opening outward, away from the "me" I have known.

☐ 41. What other people think of me is of little or *no* concern to me.

☐ 42. Having a balanced, stable, loving relationship is increasingly more important to me than achieving recognition and status.

☐ 43. I notice my body shape is changing and I'm needing to pay increased attention to nutrition and exercise in order to stay in shape.

Women

☐ 44. I have a different kind of energy—like a bird ready to spread its wings and take off with excitement.

☐ 45. I am *more* autonomous and assertive and *less* passive than I was in earlier years.

☐ 46. I am in menopause (*not* due to surgery).

☐ 47. I experience myself and others with a different, sometimes distant feeling.

☐ 48. My biological clock is ticking; I face decisions about having a child.

☐ 49. I wonder if other people see me as confused or "crazy" at times?

☐ 50. Menopause is behind me.

Men

☐ 44. My thinking seems to be shifting toward supporting and encouraging those with less experience in the workplace and/or in the community.

☐ 45. I am *more* nurturing and *less* autonomous than I was in earlier years.

☐ 46. I am having to come to terms with my body's reduced strength and endurance, increased vulnerability to disease and illness, and my shifting sense of masculinity.

☐ 47. Sometimes I find myself in periods of self-reflection about my relationship with my father in childhood.

☐ 48. I am experiencing my sexual drive with a changing sense of self; I face new decisions about partner intimacy and long-term commitment.

☐ 49. I function well outwardly most of the time, while suffering inside. I hide my turmoil and doubt.

☐ 50. My motivation and self-confidence seem to decrease as my physical abilities decline.

❖

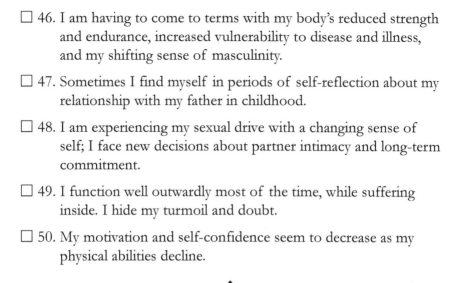

Turn the page to find out:

??? Am I in . . .

Phase 1?   **Phase 2?**   **Phase 3?**

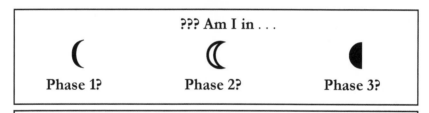

??? Which of the Seven Threads of Becoming are weaving themselves into my life at this time?

HOW TO FIND and RECORD YOUR RESULTS
(Use the Example Key below to guide you with the steps.)

Step 1: Turn the page for "The Key to the Midlife Checklist©." Find the column, at the far left, named "Checklist© Items." Work *down* the column. Circle the number of each item that you checked on your Midlife Checklist©. *(In the Example Key below items 1, 2, 4, 6, and 9 are circled.)*

Step 2: For each item you just circled, work to the right and circle each X in that row. *(See the Example Key below.)* Each X in the row relates either to a Phase of Midlife or to the Thread(s) of Becoming. Circle the Xs in each of the rows of the other Checklist© Items *you circled.*

Step 3: Find the "Phase 1" column. Work *down* the column and count up all of the **X's *that you circled*** in that column. Write the *total* for the *circled Xs* at the bottom of the column. Repeat Step 3 with the columns for "Phase 2", "Phase 3", and for each of the Seven Threads.

Checklist© Items	Phase 1	Phase 2	Phase 3	Thread A	B	C	H	I	L	R
1			X		X					X
2	X							X		
3			X	X				X	X	X
4		X		X	X			X		
5	X			X						X
6			X	X		X				
7	X						X			X
8	X				X	X			X	
9		X		X				X		
10			X		X	X				
TOTALS:	1	2	2	3	2	1	1	2	0	1

THE KEY:
MIDLIFE CHECKLIST©

Checklist© Items:	Phase 1	Phase 2	Phase 3	Thread: A	B	C	H	I	L	R
1	X							X		
2	X								X	
3		X			X		X			
4			X	X						
5			X	X						
6		X						X		
7	X								X	
8		X		X						
9			X	X						
10	X									X
11		X							X	
12			X			X				
13	X							X		
14		X						X		
15			X					X		
16			X	X				X		
17	X								X	
18	X								X	
19		X							X	
20		X						X		
21			X	X						X
22			X	X						
23	X								X	
24			X		X				X	
25		X						X		
26		X						X		

Checklist© Items:	Phase 1	Phase 2	Phase 3		Thread: A	B	C	H	I	L	R
27		X							X	X	
28		X							X		
29	X									X	
30	X								X		
31		X							X		
32	X					X					
33			X		X						
34		X									X
35	X								X		
36		X								X	
37			X		X						X
38	X									X	
39			X				X				
40	X								X		
41			X		X						
42		X						X			
43		X				X					
44		X					X	X			
45			X		X		X				
46		X				X				X	
47	X									X	
48	X					X	X				
49		X							X		
50			X			X					

TOTALS: ___ ___ ___ ___ ___ ___ ___ ___ ___ ___
      1   2   3   A   B C H I L R

☾**NOTE:** The next chapter, "My Midlife Checklist© Results," will show you which midlife phase(s) you are in and explain your results. It will define the Seven Threads of Becoming and show which of them seem most prominent in your midlife experiences now.

Chapter Five will explain the moon symbol used for the phases of midlife. It will describe in detail the characteristics of each phase of midlife and how midlife shifts us. Chapter Five also includes a discussion of the gifts that these years hold for us. Typically we do not recognize them until later in midlife and beyond.

Chapter Four

My Midlife Checklist© Results:
What Do They Mean?

A. Which Phase(s) of Midlife Am I in Now?

1. In the spaces below write your Midlife Checklist© totals for "Phases 1, 2, and 3:"

Phase 1:_____   **Phase 2:_____**   **Phase 3_____**

2. Look at your totals for the three psychological phases. Are there noticeable differences among them? Is there one total that is much greater than the others? Are there two totals that are close in size? Or, are the three totals similar?

If you have a much higher total in one phase, and a small total in each of the others, this probably means that you are living primarily in *one* of the phases of midlife at this time.

On the other hand, if your totals are quite close in two adjacent phases and very low or nonexistent in the third, it is possible that you are in a shift of sorts; there is a *noticeable* ebb and flow between the experiences of two phases. You may not be ready, yet, to leave behind or grow out of aspects of one phase, while you are growing into aspects of the next phase.

Perhaps your three totals are fairly even. If this is the case, you may be experiencing aspects of each phase, yet not living any of them fully, at this time. There may be some resistance to letting go of what was true for you in previous years but is not very true for you now. There may be feelings of self-doubt and uncertainty about where you are heading in life.

A fourth—and unlikely—pattern you might observe is one where the totals for Phases 1 and 3 are much higher than the total for Phase 2. This pattern is unlikely because, to be truly living aspects of Phase 3, one would have to have worked through many of the experiences and challenges typical of Phases 1 and 2. A richer perspective in our later midlife years comes from having done so.

This fourth pattern *may* suggest an early and very strong ambivalence about getting older. It is normal for us to feel a certain amount of ambivalence with our aging process. When it is excessive in Phase 1 over an extended period, however, we may be "stuck" in this phase and clinging to the past.

It is also possible that a high total for Phase 3 (accompanied by a high total for Phase 1 and a very low or no score for Phase 2) suggests a desire to *feel* or appear more "grown up." One may be trying out the behaviors or mannerisms associated with a wise or more mature person in midlife, while not really *experiencing* this phase within her—or himself. It is a personal rehearsal, of sorts, for what may lie ahead.

Suggestions Only

These explanations are suggestions only. They may not feel true for you. As you continue in your Midlife Check-In process, you may develop a different and more personal understanding of your Checklist results.

Chapter Five, "The Three Midlife Phases," will describe the unique aspects of each phase.

B. Which of the Seven Threads of Becoming Do My Answers Focus on *Most*?

The Midlife Checklist© Key, at the end of the previous chapter, shows how the items you checked on the instrument relate to the Seven Threads of Becoming. These are inherent in our human experience and none of us can avoid them. They weave the fabric of who and how we become, as we grow through life. Follow the directions below to record and understand your results.

Record Your Results for the Seven Threads of Becoming:

Step 1: Refer to the totals at the bottom of "The Key" on page 22 in the previous chapter. Find your totals for each of the "Thread" columns (A, B, C, H, I, L, R).

Step 2: Copy each total on its line in the list below.

Step 3: Notice which of the Seven Threads have the highest totals for you, and

Step 4: ☑ Put a check in the box by each of them:

My Results

____ ☐ Authenticity: How "real" I am in the world and with myself

____ ☐ Body: Physical changes taking place on the inside and outside of me

____ ☐ Creative Energy: Expressing myself in ways that are new and may involve risk-taking or stepping out of the box, in order to express myself in ways that are meaningful to me

____ ☐ Heart: Matters of love and intimacy

___ ☐ Identity: Sense of yourself as a presence in the world

___ ☐ Loss and Grief: Realizing and mourning the permanent passing of times, dreams, expectations, physical appearance, and people in your life

___ ☐ Relationship: Connections with others and their meaning in and for your life

---

C. Focus on One of My Threads of Becoming

1. Choose one of the Threads of Becoming that you checked on the list above. Write it here:_____

2. Refer to the Key for the Midlife Checklist© on page 22 at the end of Chapter Three. Find the item numbers in the first column on the left *that you circled*. Which of these items have an X in the column of the thread you wrote above? Highlight these items. Now, turn back to the Midlife Checklist© in Chapter Three. Find the item numbers that you just highlighted on the Key and read the statement for each of them.

✍**WONDER:** How is the thread I chose showing up in my life currently? Why are these items true for me at this time? What choices have I made or am I making in my life that affect this?

3. Turn to the Back Pocket at the end of the book and jot down your thoughts about this. (You may wish to repeat this exercise for other threads that you checked on the list above.)

✍**NOTE:** If you were to complete the Midlife Checklist© again in five to ten years, your scores for the Seven Threads of Becoming would most likely be different.

Chapter Five

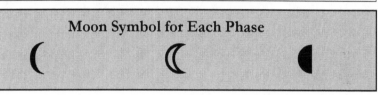

The Three Midlife Phases:
Their Moons, Meanings, Murmurings, Movement

Moon Symbol for Each Phase

You probably noticed in Chapter Four that each of the three phases of midlife is represented by a moon phase: Phase One, a crescent moon; Phase Two, a waxing moon; and Phase Three, a half moon. The moon is a meaningful symbol for the midlife phases. It has been widely revered across cultures, since ancient times, with early religious and cultural links to Nature's rhythms through life into death.

Early on, because of its apparent connection with women's menstrual cycles, called "lunar blood," it became the prime symbol of the Mother Goddess everywhere.

Various early lunar traditions associated with women continued into and throughout the Middle Ages. For their lunar holidays, the women of Christian Europe had a tradition of baking moon cakes in the shape of a crescent moon. The French called these "croissants." We enjoy them today, usually unaware of their original meaning.

In pre-Islamic Arabia, the Moon Goddess was very important. She was so important, in fact, that her emblem, the lunar crescent, was used to represent the entire country. And it still does. You can see the Moon Goddess's lunar crescent on Islamic flags today.

Meanings

When we do not have meaningful explanations for the inner stirrings and deeper shifts of our midlife years, we feel powerless. When we uncover the inherent nature of this "ground-breaking" time in life, and when we are able to deal with its multiple and varied sensations and name them or express them in meaningful ways, we are no longer powerless; we are conscious.

Your experiences in and among the three phases of midlife reflect the ebb and flow of your inner transformation process. While each phase has unique aspects that help us to recognize it, the boundaries among the phases are not firm; the shifts you experience in one phase can permeate another. This is why you can experience more than one phase at a time.

Thus, your process of transformation is not linear, moving from one phase to the next in lock-step form. Its movement is similar to the amoeba with its natural shape-shifting process. Our personal transformation evolves gradually through starts and slow-downs, detours and backtracking, outward movements and pulling inward. Our making sense of these shifting experiences does as well.

Murmurings of Each Phase

The 50 statements you read and considered on the Midlife Checklist© are "murmurings"—stirrings, feelings, concerns, and questions—that come up in us and get our attention during midlife. You checked certain statements on the Checklist as "true" for you because you resonate with them. Those are the murmurings that you recognize in your experience at this time; they are familiar. As we shift into and live awhile in a phase, our awareness of its murmurings grows deeper.

(Phase One

Phase One of midlife initiates us into a new vantage point. We typically experience this shifting in our early forties. Some individuals have glimpses of this shift in their late thirties. Our past suddenly seems very distant, our future slightly in shadow, and our present somewhat flimsy and transient. At this new place, we are caught between the worlds of our much later years and our younger ones; our values are shifting. Phase One introduces us to our midlife years, a period of transition, perplexity, and unexpected richness.

Phase One emerges in our life gradually, with a series of nudges, or it arrives abruptly, with a sudden jolt. During the few years prior to Phase One, we may have inklings or clues of subtle changes going on within us, ones we cannot yet put our finger on or tack down. In contrast, one or more life-shifting experiences, such as the unexpected loss of someone close to us, health needs of aging parents, our youngest child graduating from high school, or surgery may trigger our entry into Phase One.

Visualize a door in front of you that, when opened, brings you out of your early adult years. Imagine stepping across the threshold into a swirling mist, venturing out beyond your known world. You approach and open a door that leads you inward—into yourself—with a call to enter new, uncertain, and deepening experiences.

Phase One Murmurings

The early murmurings of Phase One lead us to wonder: How will I manage from this new vantage point, on the threshold between past and future worlds? What can I hold on to? Where am I headed? Murmurings in this phase can make us very uncomfortable; they are about changing and moving out of our comfort zone. They nudge us to redefine our sense of self and to rearrange our priorities.

In Phase One there is something happening in us at a deeper level that we have not experienced before. It feels to us that familiar ground is cracking and shifting beneath our feet. Something within us stirs and murmurs to us that our life will never be the same again. We may be bold enough to ask, "May I have my old self back, please?"

❰ Phase Two

Phase Two may emerge at any time during one's forties through late fifties. We have moved through initiation into midlife. Now we must find and draw a subtle, elusive line between who we have been and who we are now. We must consider: How will I live who I am *now*?

In this second phase of midlife, the drives of our earlier years, for money and status, are being slowly replaced by different ones, such as a more balanced life or a stable, loving relationship. As our awareness of time and mortality deepens, an urgency grows in us to accomplish things we have not yet done or attempted. Sue Monk Kidd in her book, *Travelling with Pomegranates*, describes her own experience during this phase: "In my fifties, I feel too enclosed within the walls of my small self."

Phase Two Murmurings

The majority of murmurings in Phase Two nudge us toward introspection and an examination of our life's path. Is this what I want to do for the rest of my life? Will I just keep doing this until I burn out or give up? What earlier aspirations for my life have I buried over the years that deserve my attention? Reevaluating what matters to us is paramount in Phase Two.

Before we can do this, however, we must learn to unplug ourselves from the marathon of life's demands and relationships, a major task of this phase. We must begin the process of paring down, or "pruning," the multitude of ways we focus on the outside world and create time for focusing inward.

A client of mine in Phase Two of midlife once asked me, "Have you ever ended a relationship—a friendship? There is a woman I've known and I'd like to tell her 'You're no fun anymore.' " Another client, who was in Phase Three of midlife, told me, "My life is not about keeping up. I keep things simple. I had to come to a point where the externals I'd depended upon for life had to be removed." These are examples of reevaluation and pruning.

Learning to be alone with our self, without fear, may be the most valuable result of introspective experiences in Phase Two. Personal alone time gives us the inner space we need to let ourselves drop into the questions of our midlife years.

❰ Phase Three

Phase Three usually begins sometime in our fifties or sixties. Post-menopausal women who have already grown through this phase—who have "been there"—may refer to this period of midlife as "the sweet spot." If, during their midlife years, they have been conscious of becoming who they are *really*, they have probably developed a more "real" sense of themselves and a strong sense of freedom to act on their convictions. These qualities will serve them well as they shift from their midlife years into a new phase of life.

These qualities become a part of us naturally when we focus on healthy ways to heal and grow during our ups and downs in midlife. Some of us make the conscious choice to do this inner work earlier in midlife, while others do so later on. It does not matter how old we are when we move in this direction. What matters is that we begin to heal our emotional wounds and to uncover the qualities and rich potential of the person we are meant to become. As we do so, the murmurings of Phase Three may begin.

Phase Three Murmurings

The murmurings of Phase Three build on those of Phase Two that called us into a more introspective place. Giving our self permission to have personal alone times in our busy life prepares us to shift into the "sweet spot" of midlife, the closing phase of this in-between place in life.

In this space we are not *consumed* by keeping up, making our mark, garnering financial resources, or "doing it all." Instead, more often than not, we feel a growing inner calm about where we are heading. While still difficult to accept, perhaps, we recognize the fact that death is a part of life.

Some murmurings, during the third phase, are about limiting our priorities to a few well-defined ones. We limit our relationships to those we truly enjoy or want to nurture. We engage in thoughts about who we want to become, and we let go of things we do not need or want anymore. We wonder, at times, about ways we might give back.

Phase Three murmurings call us more fervently than before to become more authentic, especially in how we express love. They move us to face conflicts with honesty and compassion.

In the third phase of midlife, something in women wants to become more autonomous and assertive than they have been. Something in men wants to become more nurturing and compassionate. The conscious choice, made earlier, to heal and grow our self from the inside out has prepared us for these murmurings. We have become more comfortable with who we are. Increasingly, what others may think of us is of little or no concern.

A restored sense of curiosity, as in a child, stirs in us during Phase Three; we explore new ideas and endeavors. Life begins to take on new fascinations for us, and we may be drawn in to explore life's mysteries. We may begin to wonder: What does my soul want of me? Feeling less "ego-directed" and more authentic or "soul-directed" is a sure sign you are shifting into this new phase and creative space of midlife, the "sweet spot."

Our Experiences Vary

Our individual experiences of moving around in the midlife phases must vary, because of our unique histories, attitudes, and circumstances. They vary, also, because of the differences among personal lifestyles.

A woman or man may be single, in a committed partnership, married, widowed, divorced, or separated. A single person may be open to multiple partners, may choose a committed relationship, have children, or prefer to live life independently.

Some individuals in midlife have young children, while others have older or grown children and some do not have children. Women and men, at any age in midlife, may be caring for elderly parents, caring for grandchildren, returning to school, shifting careers, changing committed relationships, or dealing with chronic health issues.

Thus, individual differences have a strong influence on how we choose to move through midlife and how midlife moves through us. Consider your own circumstances and lifestyle choices: How might they be affecting your perceptions and experiences in midlife at this time?

Movement: How Midlife Shifts Us

Natural Ebb and Flow

Although each phase has certain core murmurings and qualities that distinguish it from the other two, there are no sharply defined boundaries between the phases. Sometimes the phases can feel muted. Elements and experiences oscillate, and those of one phase can bleed into the next one or begin to emerge in us during a prior phase. At times, we may shift into a previous phase.

As we navigate our midlife years, an energy deep within us ebbs and flows, moving and shifting our inner world. The ocean's undercurrent does the same, sometimes in gentle ways and other times more abruptly. The continual psychological shifting deep within us is Nature's way of nudging us toward wholeness over the years.

What Moves Us to Shift

Although our midlife years are typically associated with a particular timespan (approximately 40 to late 60s), the timing of our midlife *phases* is not so predictable. Instead of there being chronological markers for midlife phases, there are physiological and psychological ones.

Physiological Markers: Hormone changes are a natural part of aging. A woman, for example, sometimes feels a shift in relation to the stage of menopause she is in: peri-menopause, menopause, or post-menopause. Postmenopausal women, as an example, may report experiencing extraordinary dreams. This indicates that significant parallel changes are taking place in the psyche.

Men, too, make physiological shifts in midlife, but their age-related hormone changes are different from those in women. The Mayo Clinic (July 23, 2011) reports that, unlike the more dramatic reproductive hormone plunge that occurs in women during menopause, sex hormone changes in men occur gradually—over a period of many years. The effects—such as changes in sexual function, energy level, or mood—tend to be subtle and sometimes can go unnoticed by men for years.

Psychological Markers: In addition to physiological shifts, we have psychological ones. We can experience a psychological shift because of an epiphany, a sudden, unexpected realization we have about an existential question, such as who am I really? or why am I here? We experience other psychological shifts when we do the work to heal ourselves from the inside out.

Bird's-Eye-View:
Shifts and Overlaps

The illustration below is a bird's-eye-view of how and when our midlife phases may merge or overlap. Keep in mind the fluid-like quality of the phases and the fact that everyone's midlife journey is unique. If this example does not represent your experience, draw in what seems to be true for you.

Possible Merging and Overlap of Midlife Phases

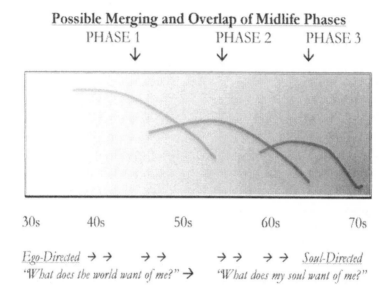

NOTE: The gradiance in shading represents deepening awareness of one's mortality and the limited time one has.

The Gifts of Midlife

In our early years of midlife, we are unaware of many gifts inherent in this period of our life that hide in the spaces of our experience. It is in our gradual and deepening process of self-knowing and self-awareness that we are increasingly able to see them. Some of the gifts of our midlife years relate directly to the brain's vitality and the positive shifts that are taking place in it. Other gifts relate to our increasing psychological resilience.

Brain Vitality and Positive Shifts

Our brain is alive and well during our midlife years. In fact, it continues to grow new brain cells throughout life. It reshapes itself as we engage in new learning and life experiences. We promote memory resilience when we make healthy choices in exercise, nutrition, sleep hygiene, social engagement and mind challenges.

As we move through our midlife years and on, we are increasingly able to develop a more balanced perspective on life because, as we age, we tend to increase our use of both sides of our brain for cognition. We merge the logical, language thinking hemisphere with the creative, synthesizing hemisphere to solve problems and make decisions. In addition, the brain centers that process emotions mature and mellow and our limbic (emotional) system grows calmer. As a result, we experience more positive and less negative emotions.

Psychological Resilience

Psychologically and emotionally, we become more resilient as we grow through our midlife phases and beyond. We are building toward increased fortitude. For example, we get better at letting go of the limiting defenses and strategies that have undermined our authenticity. Also, as we mature into our midlife experience, we begin to have a sense of control over events in our lives. We are less compelled to repeat self-defeating patterns of behavior. The interesting fact is that most people in midlife use the word "challenges," instead of "crises," to describe their difficulties. The idea of "meeting the challenge" energizes them. Our maturing middle-aged mind prompts us to *do* something about a difficulty, rather than despair about it. It is not a crisis; it is a challenge.

Another gift we reap in these years is that we become less alienated from our feelings and more in tune with what is real in us. Our growing resiliency contributes to our stronger sense of personal identity and increased confidence.

A wealth of life experience is being encoded in our brains as we move through our midlife years. We draw on it, increasingly, to help us make decisions and address problems.

All of the gifts that we cannot see earlier in our midlife years become apparent to us gradually as we open, more and more, to becoming who we are *really*.

It Matters How We Respond to Midlife

As we navigate our midlife phases, we face the convergence of many life conditions and circumstances, some from our past and others more recent. Some of us will respond to this challenge in ways that bring insight, emotional healing, and personal growth.

Others will work hard to resist the changes that midlife brings; they will cling to what is slipping away. As a result, they may become emotionally "stuck." A client, age fifty-eight, had come to therapy to resolve some emotional wounds from her childhood. As we neared the closing of our work together, she described her experience of having been "stuck" for so many years: "As long as I was holding on to it (old hurt), I couldn't let it flow by me." Depending on how long one's resistance continues in life, an individual could remain stuck for years.

How we manage our midlife experiences is critical for our growth and development during midlife. And it is critical for another very important reason: How we live and grow in our midlife years will determine *how we experience life in our later years.*

**Midlife Glossary:
Check Out These Words**

Below is a list of glossary words you may wish to explore in relation to this chapter. ☑ Put a check by any that "call" to you, and find their meanings in the Midlife Glossary. How might the words relate to *the phase(s) of midlife you are in at this time?*

☐ acceptance

☐ autobiographical self

☐ menopausal transition

☐ midlife

☐ self-worth

☐ suffering

☐ wisdom

Chapter Six

"Your experience and ways of expressing
are the real life you live."
John O'Donohue

The Seven Threads of Becoming weave themselves continuously in and out of our lives. They are facets of the human experience that we cannot escape. Every question we ponder, choice we make, and action we live is tied to one or more of these seven threads. They weave the fabric of who and how we become as we grow through life. The Seven Threads of Becoming include: **A**uthenticity, **B**ody, **C**reative Energy, **H**eart Matters, **I**dentity, **L**oss and Grief, and **R**elationship. The threads never change; our experiences with them do.

Each of these threads weaves colors more brightly or subtly in different times and circumstances of our life. The intensity of color and the patterns they make reflect our inner and outer responses to life. They will vary depending on our maturity and the stage of life we are in. What we focus on in one stage of life can be forgotten or become less important during another stage, when new uncertainties, interests, and experiences take their place.

Sometimes a deeper concern or some "unfinished business" is hidden in the weaving. A particular concern may linger in us, for many years, and hide in the fabric of "other things" we are focused on. At some point (often in midlife), something in us brings the concern to center stage; it demands our attention. That "something," for example, may be health issues or relationship turmoil that we can no longer ignore. It may be grief that was never processed in healthy ways and now expresses itself as anger. It may be about something we did that we are ashamed of. That "something" may also be an annoying unrest inside of us seeking change. We often become more conscious of these hidden issues when deeper questions and uncomfortable circumstances begin shifting us inside. Our depths have a way of working us.

Some threads become frayed over time due to repeated experiences as well as lessons we still need to learn. Some of these threads are "loose" and we need to reweave them into our fabric of becoming in new and more authentic ways. When we do this, we strengthen our process of growing toward wholeness, our true Self. We move into becoming more of who we are meant to be.

Some threads weave themselves into our life experience more intensely during midlife, when inner and outer psychological shifts may be "rocking our boat." Most of the issues we encounter in these years relate to the two overarching tasks of midlife and later years: 1) a search for meaning—for making sense of one's self and life, and 2) personal transformation—the invisible inner process of growing toward wholeness. Your Midlife Check-In process engages you with these tasks directly in Parts Three and Four of the book.

The list below, "What Comes Up Often in Midlife," connects typical changes, issues, and focal points of our middle passage to the Seven Threads of Becoming. The items on the list emerge in us naturally as part of our human experience of transformation. These concerns and circumstances get our attention in order to grow us.

Read through the list. Put a ✔ by any items that ring true for you at this time, whether in positive or negative ways. Notice which of the seven thread(s) the items you checked connect with. You may want to add changes or concerns in your own experience that are not on this list.

WHAT COMES UP OFTEN IN MIDLIFE?
Typical Issues, Changes, Focal Points
Related to the Seven Threads of Becoming

Authenticity Thread

___ Acceptance of who I am
___ Letting go (of earlier ambitions, lifestyle, youthful ideals, superficial relationships, others' expectations, etc.)
___ Needing clarity for meaningful direction in life
___ Elimination of toxic influences in my life
___ What draws me so deeply into life and into my own nature
___ Encountering unexpressed parts of who I am
___ Seeking inner joy
___ What others think of me

Body Thread

___ Visible physical changes
___ Changes in energy, physical strength, and well-being
___ Peri-menopause, menopause, post-menopause
___ Mortality and dying
___ Image, identity, public impression concerns
___ Illness and disease
___ Biological clock
___ Cloudy thinking

Creative Energy Thread

___ Mood (e.g. lack of inspiration, mood fluctuation)
___ Clarity about where I am heading in my life
___ Buried energy wanting to express itself
___ Low self-confidence
___ Imagining something different
___ Time for play

Heart Thread

__ Wanting to control or change others and outcomes
__ Feeling "lost"
__ Confusion about what matters
__ Decisions about partner intimacy and commitment
__ Connecting with my feelings, passions, and/or spiritual
beliefs
__ Unhealed emotional wounds
__ Forgiveness

Identity Thread

__ Feeling caught between two lives
__ Finding who I am at a deeper level
__ Accepting my uniqueness and difference from others
__ Being mortal
__ Generation values
__ Role conflict or confusion (e.g. parenting a parent)
__ Suffering inside while functioning well outwardly

Loss and Grief Thread

__ Painful memories and their effects
__ Changing roles
__ Reduced self-confidence and motivation
__ Body aging and mortality
__ Leaving behind a younger identity and lifestyle
__ Deaths of others
__ Regrets about earlier choices and decisions
__ Leaving behind my capability of bearing a child
__ Diminishing sexual drive

Relationship Thread

___ Shifts within a committed relationship
___ Forgiveness of others
___ Seeking new relationships
___ Becoming more nurturing
___ Trust and fidelity
___ Partners' differences in age and stage-of-life
___ Adult children
___ Families of adult children
___ Assuming a parenting role for my parents or other elders
___ Becoming a mentor or support person for others
___ Balance and stability in a loving relationship

If you are currently working with a therapist or considering doing so, this exercise can be a useful self-assessment to share.

Midlife Glossary:
Check Out These Words

    Below is a list of glossary words you may wish to explore in relation to this chapter. ☑ Put a check by any that "call" to you, and find their meanings in the Midlife Glossary. How might the words relate to *the Threads of Becoming weaving themselves into your life at this time?*

☐ false self

☐ meaning

☐ midlife crisis

☐ soul

☐ tasks

☐ trait

Chapter Seven

*Ah . . . . . an important question, and one that deserves an honest answer:
As your midlife journey begins to ebb, your full-moon phase begins to flow,
leading you toward the gift of a deeper, more heartful connection with your
purpose in life.*

When you come to grips with most of your mid-life challenges
and ambivalent feelings, and when you adjust, more-or-less, to
life-with-mortality, Nature gives you a psychological nudge, once again,
and beckons you to enter the full-moon phase of your life.

The core question of the full-moon phase lurks in the shadows
while you journey through the forest of midlife. When the time comes
for you to leave the forest, this question will step out into the light and
confront you. It will ask: *"What is the meaning of my life?"*

When we explore the meaning of our life, in the light of the full
moon, thoughts and insights can emerge and take form in unexpected
ways. They may arrive in the curling tails of ethereal mist, on wafting
strands of a passing breeze, or in the power of someone's example.
Your life may make more sense to you in isolated moments; insights

may pop into your mind suddenly like the "poof" of an umbrella when it opens all at once.

The timing of this next shift in your life will depend on the choices and decisions you make now, in your midlife years. Perhaps the advice below, offered by several full-moon women, will provide inspiration for some of your choices and decisions at this time in your life?

O
Advice from Full-Moon Women

"Pick friends whose advice you can trust, who you can laugh with, and drink a little wine with. Be true to yourself and bloom where planted."
Francie (and Friends), Full-Moon Woman, age 79

Advice like this comes from twenty-one Traditionalists (women born from 1922-1942) and Golden Baby Boomers (1943-1947) who completed a five-item questionnaire as part of my background work for this book. I wanted to provide perspectives and advice of women who have "been there" before you.

Of course, the midlife years you are living are not the same ones your parents or grandparents lived. The backdrop of current events, political issues, lifespan expectancies, and changing norms for women, families, and lifestyles differ from previous generations. Nonetheless, Nature's intent for becoming who we are meant to be remains constant, and the psychological and physiological shifts of midlife are her way of accomplishing this.

The five-item questionnaire was distributed to women in various settings and communities by individuals to friends in distant places, by friends of friends, and by women in classes and book groups. Each woman gave candid information about her midlife experience. Each one also gave a "piece of advice" for women currently living their midlife years, based on what they can "see" *now* but could not have seen during the time of their own midlife journey. They gave their advice, knowing that it might be quoted in this book.

The stories these women shared are diverse and varied. Several of them who have had long-term relationships remarked on the great value of their spouse's love and support; others had found that the marriage they had been in prior to midlife was no longer meaningful or empowering as they moved into their middle years. These women discovered, through career decisions and divorce, their individual resourcefulness and abilities to meet challenges head-on. This led them to new self-confidence and self-understanding about what mattered to them in their lives, ultimately. They were living more of their true Self.

Several women mentioned that specialized training or professional endeavors in midlife helped give them a sense of purpose and prepared them for new endeavors in their later years. Looking back, many of the women came to realize how their healthy risk-taking in midlife was essential to their personal growth for years following. The primary form of risk-taking was leaving non-meaningful relationships. Others were returning to school, becoming a professional, or pursuing a personal interest seriously.

While my sample of responses is small and cannot represent all women 70 and older, I believe the advice of the women quoted here may be useful and inspiring to readers.

The advice of these full-moon women relates to nine ideas. I hope that, among the quoted pieces of advice below, you will find just the inspiration you may need for your journey!

Love Yourself. Be True to Yourself

"Love yourself as well as others." *Peggy, 81*
"Follow your passion, dream, and be grateful each day." *Claire, 77*
"Be lovingly, compassionately, true to yourself." *Barbara, 90*

Resist Limitations; Stay Open to Possibilities

"Try to let go of your preconceived notion of what you can and cannot do and of who you think you are. You might be surprised and happy with who you turn out to be and with what you can do, and be proud of the difference!"

Merrylee, 72

"Keep your dreams and options open, while you also tend to the important relationships and meaningful work that falls to you."

Linda, 72

Choose Friends Wisely

"Spend time with women you admire and learn from them." *Carole, 70*

"Pick friends whose advice you can trust." *Francie, 79*

Be Positive, Be Brave, Be Active

"Be positive and strong! Set goals to accomplish." *Linda, 72*

"Hang in there!" *Ruth, 83*

"Be active and enjoy friends." *Shirley, 96*

"Find something to do that brings sustainable meaning to your life—something you can pursue until you die. And always give back to the community." *Claire, 77*

"Be brave even when you may feel fear." *Carole, 70*

"Persevere." *Francie, 79*

Be in the Present

"Each moment is a gift. Enjoy each breath as
though it could be your last." *Ellen, 74*

"Enjoy every day and every experience.
Laugh a lot, stay present, and dance!" *Pat, 77*

Get Out of Your Comfort Zone

"Get out of your comfort zone. Try new things—classes, groups, painting.
Who knows what will inspire you." *Barbara, 78*

Learn from Difficulties

"Adversity is to learn from, to improve life." *Pat, 81*

Strengthen Your Inner Resources

"If you're concerned about soul, spirit, and Self, you can rise above the
difficulties of the aging process." *Barbara, 72*

Risk Moving On

"Ask yourself if your current lifestyle is working for you and is what
you want to continue. If <u>not</u>, then dare to take the risk to move on."

Barbara, 81

Who knows what will evolve for *you* in the full moon phase? We do
know that the road winds on into a journey of the soul. And that,
Dear Reader, is the subject of a different book.

Midlife Glossary:
Check Out These Words

Below is a list of glossary words you may wish to explore in relation to this chapter. ☑ Put a check by any that "call" to you, and find their meanings in the Midlife Glossary. How might the words relate to *how you imagine yourself being in your full-moon years?*

☐ aging

☐ authenticity

☐ full-moon phase

☐ self-awareness

☐ tree (as symbol)

☐ true Self

THREE

The Three Urgent Questions of Midlife

&

&

&

Introduction

Chapter Eight
Who Have I Been?

Chapter Nine
Who Am I Now?

Chapter Ten
Who Am I *Really*?

"Try to let go of your preconceived notion of what you can and cannot do and of who you think you are. You might be surprised and happy with who you turn out to be and with what you can do—and be proud of the difference!!

Merrylee, Full-Moon Woman, 72

Introduction

1. Who have I been?
2. Who am I now?
3. Who am I *really*?

These three questions swim around in us at different times in our life. In midlife, these questions push themselves up to the surface and get our attention with a new kind of urgency. Sometimes, we feel just the slightest hint of their presence; at other times, these questions hit us head-on. They do not give up, they push at us from within, and they insist on honest answers.

And, honesty *is* the best policy! The kind of relationship you develop with these three questions during midlife will have a direct effect on how you experience life in your later years.

<u>**Each chapter in Part Three focuses on one of the three urgent questions. You will work with these core sections in each chapter:**</u>

- Focusing on the Positives
- Exploring My Identity
- Digging Deeper
- Checking In: My Comfort Level and Feelings
- Midlife Glossary Words: Check These Out
- Sitting Under (Or Leaning Against) My Midlife Tree

✐ NOTE:

As you work with the exercises in each chapter, you will be gathering the information and personal insights you need for considering who and how you want to become. My experience is that some of the topics and exercises in each chapter could tap into some difficult subjects and experiences.

Here are three suggestions for handling uncomfortable emotions that may come up:

• Stop the exercise, take a few *slow* belly breaths, and turn to the Feelings Gauge and the list of 21 ways you can take care of yourself in the moment. Choose one or more.

• Change your physical position. For example, if you are seated, stand up, stretch, and walk; if you are lying down, roll over or get up and stretch. Then, move your body freely to release tension and relax yourself.

• If your discomfort continues, you may want to seek the support of a mental health professional.

✐

Chapter Eight

Who Have I Been?

"Open your head like an egg and, in a state of healthy superiority, wonder about yourself."
Erik Satie

"Who have I *been*?" is a question we ask when we begin noticing that parts of our life and parts of *us* are changing. Pieces of our identity that we have put together over the years are coming loose. The ground on which we have staked our identity is shifting; we are increasingly off-balance in relationships, priorities, and inside of ourselves. What we have known and have assumed would remain in place is sliding out from under us; uncertainty is the placeholder. We are entering new territory . . .

Our fear of losing who we *thought* we were can make the question "who have I been" seem urgent. While our fear may drive us to hold on tight to the identity or story we know and have lived, it can also awaken the question in us. And when we begin to focus on this question, we also begin the powerful adult journey of gathering meaning for our life and understanding who we are. Finding important pieces of our past experiences is essential to this journey.

Remembering who we have been is a process of discovery, one that will continue into our later years. When we remember, we go back and excavate the years that came before. We recall images, connect feelings with our experiences, and put pieces together. We give new meaning to things we knew before.

The way we characterize our past experiences deeply influences how satisfied we are with our current life. Notice any judgments, positive or negative, that you make about your past experiences as you work within this chapter. Then consider your level of satisfaction in your life today.

I recommend that you take a few minutes, at the conclusion of this chapter, to sit under your personal Tree of Midlife and reflect on "Who have I been?" <u>Consider:</u> *What captured my attention most? What puzzled or concerned me? What do I want to explore further? How does who I have been influence or affect my life today?* What colors and patterns did your Threads of Becoming weave into who you have been?

Record the thoughts, questions, and insights that come to you, about who you have been, in your personal notebook or in the Back Pocket at the very end of the book. You may wish to follow this, at some point, with other forms of expression about who you have been: music, drawing, collage, painting, creative movement, poetry or other creative writing.

I believe that, in the end, after you have read and worked with the exercises, some of the most valuable insights about who you have been will come from your time of relaxed and thoughtful reflection under the tree.

In this chapter, you will increase your understanding of who you have been. You will:

- Glance back at meaningful points in time
- Focus on the positives
- Explore your past identity
- Dig deeper

You will have the opportunity to check in with your comfort level and your feelings with the "Where Am I?" and "Feelings Gauge" exercises.

In addition, you may wish to extend your knowledge and deepen your understanding of midlife by exploring "Midlife Glossary: Check Out These Words." Find their meanings in the Midlife Glossary.

✍ **NOTE:** *If, at any time, while engaging in this chapter, you do not feel comfortable with what comes up, turn to "21 Ways to Take Care of Myself Right Now" on page 87 and follow the directions. Take a break. Check in with a professional if your discomfort continues and interferes with your daily functioning.*

Glancing Back
At Meaningful Points in Time

- Getting Started: Charting Your Pre-Midlife Years
  - A Meaningful Year in My Past

GETTING STARTED:
Charting Your Pre-Midlife Years

Think of your adolescent (approximately 12-21), young adult (22-28), and early adult (29-39) years as a calendar of events. Now look at the timelines on the next three pages. The first timeline represents the years in your life as you remember them from age 39 to age 29. The second timeline represents the ages from age 28 to age 22. The third timeline is for ages 21 to 12.

Look over the years on each timeline. Put a star on the line for an event or experience that happened when you were a certain age AND that felt significant to you *at the time*. An event may have stood out for both positive or negative reasons at the time. It may have been pleasant or unpleasant for you. It may have been especially fun or memorable (such as an honor, an important goal, or a turning point).

These events can be big or small; they can be things you did alone or with others. Only you can decide which events feel important enough to star. If you get stuck trying to remember "significant" events in your life, say to yourself: "I am (#) years old. What has happened in my life during this age?"

When you finish marking the timelines, ask, "Which of the events that I thought were significant, at the time, seem *less* important to me now?" "Which ones have I let go of?" And, "Which ones do I want to revisit and clarify?"

Charting Your Pre-Midlife Years:
Early Adult Years

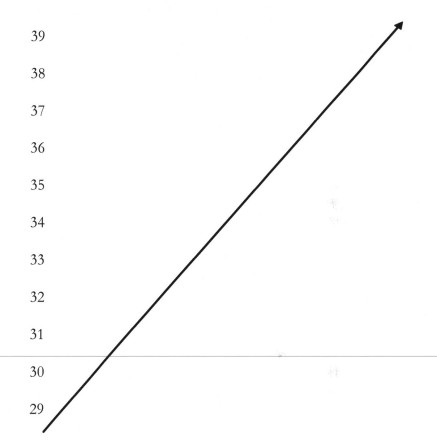

39

38

37

36

35

34

33

32

31

30

29

Charting Your Pre-Midlife Years:
Young Adult Years

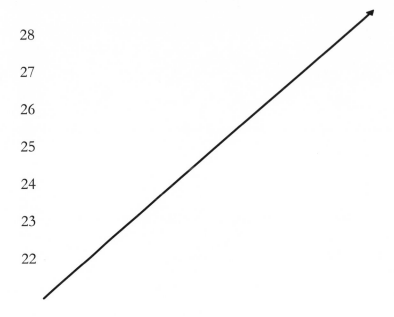

28

27

26

25

24

23

22

Charting Your Pre-Midlife Years:
Adolescent Years

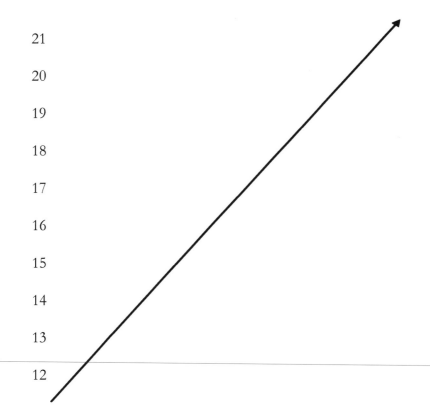

21

20

19

18

17

16

15

14

13

12

A MEANINGFUL YEAR IN MY PAST

As you look back, there may be certain years with special importance and meaning for you. In this exercise, you will reflect on one of those years. After you choose a year, use the following outline to note your reflections.

The year of_____was a very important year for me.

I

_____

_____

_____

_____

And

_____

_____

_____

Finally,

_____

_____

_____

And so

_____

_____

_____

_____

Focusing on the Positives

- My Golden Nuggets
- My Story: Capturing a Positive Experience
from My Past

MY GOLDEN NUGGETS:
Gifts from My Pre-Midlife Years

When we realize that our ever-so-familiar life and rhythms are changing, both outside *and* inside of ourselves, a feeling of loss moves in. Some of us may worry and fret over these changes; we may fear the unknown. Others of us may experience the relief of moving on!

Instead of putting our attention on what we have lost or missed, however, why not put our attention on what might be *found* in the story we have been living? For example, we have learned lessons and acquired skills that have helped us navigate in life; we have created and ended relationships, and we have achieved goals. In living our story, we have shared love, overcome obstacles, and endured pain that has shattered and strengthened us.

While loss of time, people, body image, and facility are parts of our aging process, the *gains* we have are considerable. These gains are the golden nuggets from our past that we can mine during midlife and beyond; no one can put a price on them!

What valuable resources have been woven into the fabric of *your* story? Take stock of the assets to be mined from your experiences. Do they include special knowledge or expertise? Specific skills? Courage to act? Compassion? Risks taken? Valuable insights? Healthy boundaries? Lessons learned in relationships?

Midlife is the opportunity to draw upon these assets, for their benefits now and in the future. In midlife, there are different kinds of decisions to make and obstacles to manage; there are unexpected changes to adjust to, and different kinds of challenges to meet. In the midlife years, there are joys, delightful surprises, and new pursuits ahead that you could not have planned for or experienced in earlier years.

Like a savings account, the cache of golden nuggets you have built up is available for you to use. When you draw on these personal assets, their value increases, and you add value to your life.

On the lines below, name some golden nuggets, from your past, that you are mining in midlife:

☐ _____

☐ _____

☐ _____

☐ _____

☐ _____

Put a ☑ by the "nuggets" that are especially valuable to you.

CONSIDER:

What might the nuggets you checked reveal to you about the strengths, skills, attitudes, motivation, courage, and/or knowledge that you developed in previous years of your life?

_____

_____

_____

_____

MY STORY:
Capturing a Positive Experience from My Past

Think back to an experience, from earlier years, that had a positive influence on you. Perhaps this experience held an important lesson for you or taught you a skill that helped you succeed. It might have been an experience through which you discovered something important—about yourself, someone else, or about life. Or, this experience may have led you into a life-long interest. Whatever the reason may be that you think of it as positive, this experience is an important part of the story of who you have been.

How might you capture this experience in order to bring it to life for yourself or for others? Here are four suggestions:

1. Tell the story of this experience to others. Tell it to someone who is younger, such as an adolescent or an adult child.

2. Write about the experience. If there happen to be photos related to it, put them and your written version together.

3. Choose theme music for the experience. As you listen to this music, reflect on the positive aspects of the experience.

4. Identify images and objects that, for you, capture the essence of the experience you have chosen.

When you communicate your positive experience in one of these ways, you bring it to life and make it available for personal reflection. Sharing your story from past years with another person can link both of you in a heart-filled way. It can give someone a glimpse into who you have been, and help that person understand more about who you are now.

Exploring My Identity

- My Identity in the Past
- My Identity: Assumed or Real?
- A Symbol of Who I Have Been

MY IDENTITY IN THE PAST

Your sense of identity in your 20s and 30s was associated with various self-images, ideals, hopes, goals, voices, roles, and expectations. What were some of these for you? Who did you believe you were—as a presence in the world? Use the following prompts to help you gather ideas:

- Positive or negative self-images and role models that helped me to define myself in my 20s and 30s:

_____

_____

_____

- Hopes, dreams, or ideals I aspired to in my 20s and 30s:

_____

_____

_____

- Goals I set:

_____

_____

_____

- How I used my voice *most of the time* (e.g. giving in or consenting, speaking out, writing, rebelling, whining, persuading, helping others, making decisions on my own, keeping quiet, partnering with others, making peace, creating art, performing):

_____

_____

_____

- The message I most wanted to communicate was:

_____

_____

_____

• The main roles (e.g. student, caring family supporter, dutiful child, rebellious one or tough kid, "parent," loyal friend, quiet one, active community member, peace maker,loving spouse or partner, leader, social butterfly, jock, outcast, jokester, loner, etc.) that I played in my life during previous years were:

_____

_____

_____

• The following two or three people had an important influence on who I have been (family member, friend, teacher, mentor, co-worker, spouse, lover):

_____

_____

_____

• Expectations I had for myself included:

_____

_____

_____

(Were these expectations *yours*—or *someone else's?*)

CONSIDER:

• Was there a time when you began to feel that the identity you were living was no longer working *for* you?

_____

_____

_____

• Is the persona I was living before the one I want to continue living now and in the future? Which parts of it might I want to keep? Let go of?

KEEP:

_____

_____

_____

LET GO OF:

_____

_____

_____

• There may be someone or something special you have left behind. What feelings come forward when you consider this?

_____

_____

_____

🖉 **NOTE:** *Simply acknowledging the feelings contributes to your inner health.*

MY IDENTITY:
Assumed or Real?

When we are children and the adults in our lives feel uncomfortable with who we are naturally, they convey their discomfort with various responses and messages. Some of the messages adults give a child early in life can actually motivate the child to push aside who he or she really is in favor of a persona based on the adult's "shoulds." Assuming this mask helps the child to avoid the rejection which comes through criticism, blame, and conflict. It also pushes underground the young person's true vitality, needs, and feelings.

Perhaps pushing away deeper needs and feelings is a familiar experience of your own childhood? Adults in your life may have said things to you like: "Don't be angry; it's not nice to be angry," "Who do you think you are with an idea like that?" "Pay attention to your looks and you'll go far," "Be quiet and don't complain," "Do what I tell you," "Big boys don't cry," "Girls don't do that," "You'll never amount to anything," "What do you mean you want to be an artist? You can't make any money doing that!" "Don't embarrass us," and, especially, "You shouldn't feel that way."

These kinds of messages can lead us to repress, or hold back, our natural vitality, in order to feel acceptable, and to become the someone others said we "should" be. This persona feels safer; it helps us to avoid painful criticism, blame, and conflict. Our self-sabotage, however, moves us away from expressing our true spirit and fullness. We may be living a "safe" life, but without feeling our true joy and expressing our deeper needs. Our fears and defenses separate us from expressing our true Self in the world.

CONSIDER:

How true might this be for you? Are there parts of yourself that went underground which you would like to retrieve or heal? When did you stop singing and dancing?

A SYMBOL OF WHO I HAVE BEEN

There are times when we have a feeling about something but words are not enough to convey that feeling. An experience may touch or move us deeply, or some deeper place in us "knows" what we mean but does not have words to express it.

A symbol can help us capture the meaning without relying on words. A "symbol" is something that represents something else by association or resemblance. Often it is a material object used to represent something invisible like a concept, a meaning, or a feeling. A symbol can also be a graphic design, or a physical gesture, such as a handshake, a nod, a respectful bow, or a salute.

Consider the abundance of symbols we have in advertising, religions, and in our possessions. In your own experience, think of the products, religious images, decorative pieces, or souvenirs that matter to you because of the *meaning* you relate to them. Each item may have a name, but it is what the item *represents* that "speaks" to you and not the words. You see an image, hear a particular sound, or see someone's gesture and you "get" its symbolic meaning.

Consider "Who" You Have Been

While you were working with the focus question in this chapter, certain feelings, beliefs, energy, and/or values about who you have been may have emerged in you. What inner sense do you have of yourself? What symbol that you know (or might create) could represent the deeper meaning or sense you have of who you have been?

If nothing comes to mind, look around your environments for objects and ideas. What items or images with special meaning for you have you chosen for your home and work environments? Browse magazines and online image collections. Look at designs on book covers. Look at images in nature. What jumps out at you? What may hold some or all of the meaning for you of who you have been?

Choose something. Make a note of it, or put the image in your Back Pocket or personal notebook. Would you like to give it a descriptive name, or is the image enough?

Digging Deeper

- Ten Below
- Notice and Reflect
- Holes and Empty Places:
  Unmet Needs from My Past

TEN BELOW

The 10 statements below can help you dig deeper and respond to the question, "Who have I been?" You may or may not have considered some of these ideas before.

As you read each statement, be spontaneous; fill in what comes to mind first. If you cannot think of something to write, go on to the remaining items and come back. The best approach is to work from your gut. The best policy is honesty. Remember: this is for YOU!

☐ **1.** A positive experience of earlier years I would love to relive is

_____

_____

_____

☐ **2.** I followed my heart and was true to myself when I

_____

_____

_____

☐ **3.** _____
has mattered deeply to me most of my life.

☐ **4.** For me, feeling loved has always been

_____

_____

_____

☐ **5.** An important lesson I learned many years ago is

_____

_____

_____

☐ **6.** A major obstacle or "hard place" I overcame in my younger
years is

_____

_____

_____

☐ **7.** Three personal strengths that have served me well over the
years include

_____

_____

_____

☐ **8.** A habit or practice of mine that has interfered negatively with
my life over the years has been

_____

_____

_____

☐ **9.** It has always been hard for me to

_____

_____

_____

☐ **10.** An experience in my youth that I have never shared with
anyone and would like to let go of is

_____

_____

_____

⌇ NOTICE and REFLECT

Review the 10 statements you completed above:

Notice:

• Which statements were easy for you to answer?
• Which statements were especially difficult for you to answer?
☑Put a check next to them.

✄ **NOTE:** *A strong, uncomfortable reaction to completing a statement may suggest that something in you cries out for mending; there may be "unfinished business" that needs healing resolution. If so, seeking professional support may be appropriate for you.*

Reflect:

Do any concerns call out to you to be resolved? If you keep a journal, work with the arts, or have a meditation practice or other quiet time, consider using one of the statements that you checked above as a focus for reflection.

✎Jot down what you notice about your responses:

_____

_____

_____

_____

HOLES AND EMPTY PLACES:
Unmet Needs From My Past

✍ **NOTE**: *If you are currently dealing with a personal crisis or another emotional upheaval, please consider working on the following exercise in partnership with a licensed therapist. Or, come back to this when you feel grounded.*

Your answers to "Who have I been?" would not be complete without considering the holes and empty places that may have been left inside of you early on in life. These "holes" are unmet emotional needs, and they are critical to an understanding of who you have been.

Our basic emotional needs include:

- feeling loved
- feeling we belong
- feeling safe
- feeling worthy

When these needs are not met, there are holes and empty places inside of us. Loss, rejection, longing, and unfulfilled dreams can generate these spaces.

For example, having been loved for what we *achieve* (vs. for simply being ourself) may have left an empty place in us; the loss of a beloved individual may have left a different emotional hole in us. In some of our lives, there may be an empty place in our self-worth, due to frequent rejection by others. A hole in our sense of self may have developed if we followed the plan that others had laid out for our life, *instead of* pursuing the plan that excited us.

Holes and Empty Places Speak to Us

Each of us has our own emotional "holes" and empty places created by unmet needs. We may be aware of some of them and unaware of others. Whether they appear on our radar screen or not, these inner voids speak to us.

Holes and empty places "speak" through the painful feelings and negative beliefs we acquired earlier in life. These feelings and beliefs are tangible expressions of our unmet fundamental needs. Feelings such as deep disappointment, low self-worth, long-held anger, hopelessness, a longing to be seen or heard, and the fear of telling our truth are echoes from empty places.

Negative Beliefs and Self-Doubts

The list below includes some of the negative beliefs and self-doubts that reflect our unmet emotional needs:

___ "It is not ok for me to fail at anything."
___ "No one really cares about me."
___ "It's risky to trust other people."
___ "No matter what I do, I cannot win."
___ "I don't have a choice."
___ "I don't deserve love."
___ "I'm not lovable."
___ "I have no control in my life."
___ "Anything less than perfect is not good enough."
___ "I'm not safe."
___ "I don't belong."

Do any of these painful feelings and negative beliefs (or others not mentioned here) feel familiar to you? ☑ Put a check next to them or note them on the lines below:

_____

_____

_____

What unmet emotional need(s) might these painful feelings or negative beliefs be echoing from your past? The need to feel loved? To feel that you belong? To feel safe? To feel worthy?

✐ Possible Unmet Needs

Unmet need: _____

Unmet need: _____

Unmet need: _____

What Fills the Holes?

When any of the fundamental emotional needs of love and belonging, safety, and worthiness have not been met in us, feelings of disappointment, anger, fear, and low self-worth usually move in and fill these empty places. These feelings, however, do not grow us toward fulfillment and well-being. They keep us stuck.

When one or more of our basic emotional needs is not met, our instincts at a deeper level prompt us to get that need met. This natural drive to feel love, safety, belonging, or worthiness, however, may lead us to adopt *un*healthy strategies for getting our needs met.

Five Unhealthy Strategies We May Adopt In Order to Get Our Emotional Needs Met

1. Working hard to please others
2. Manipulating others
3. Playing the "victim"
4. Taking on responsibility for others' choices
5. Distancing our self from others, physically or emotionally

When we use these unhealthy strategies, we cut ourselves off from our feelings. We develop a persona and hope others will respond in ways that will meet our emotional need. For example, if our unmet need is to feel loved, we may work hard to "get" love by working hard to *please others*.

If the unmet need we have is to feel validated and to have a sense of personal power, we may learn to *manipulate others*, in order to experience these feelings.

We may have felt rejected often in our youth and may not have had a sense of belonging. As a result, we may have taken on the *"victim" role*, a strategy for getting the attention and connection we craved.

Perhaps, while growing up, we were the one who was blamed when things did not turn out well. If so, our sense of self-worth may have a hole in it somewhere. We may still believe that it is our fault—that we are responsible—when things don't work out well. Therefore, to increase the chances that things *will* turn out well (and to feel a positive sense of self), our strategy may have been to *become the "responsible one,"* and to take control by taking care of others, or taking credit or blame for their choices and decisions.

A sense of safety is a fundamental need. Some of us grew up feeling unsafe in our family or in the larger world. If so, and in order to feel safe, we might have used one or more of the strategies below:

Four Unhealthy Strategies We May Use In Order to Feel Safe

1. Create emotional or physical distance between us and others
2. Try to be like others and live a false self or wear a persona or mask
3. Refrain from expressing anger because it is not "nice"
4. Strive to achieve the "right" weight and appearance in order to feel acceptable.

Holes and Empty Places Are Openings to Growth

We can think of the holes and empty places we may have inside as hidden or closed off dark places without hope or possibility. *Or,* we can think of these places as *openings* or portals for us to step through into healthy opportunities for personal growth. The threshold of a portal is like a bridge. It connects our past experiences of emotional wounding with possibilities for healing. It can also be a bridge between our negative self-beliefs and more positive ones.

When we become aware of an unmet need and any unhealthy strategies we use to get our needs met, we are close to stepping through the opening. Being aware of our unmet needs and unhealthy strategies is essential for healing emotional wounds, strengthening our sense of self-worth, and deepening our compassion for self and for others. They are essential for becoming more authentic.

These opportunities for personal growth may not be recognizable at first glance; they may show up in a disguise. For example, some opportunities show up in the form of a challenge, such as the challenge to face a fear. When someone asks for your help, this may be an opportunity to heal anger, disappointment, or low self-worth. A person who wants to reconcile differences with you provides another chance for you to begin healing.

When we accept a challenge to overcome something that has held us back, when we extend our self to others, and when we make amends to others, we are using healthy strategies for healing our unmet emotional needs. In the process, we are strengthening our sense of self-worth and deepening our compassion for self and for others.

You will discover these kinds of opportunities for healing and for strengthening your character and compassion by being on the lookout for them. The choice of whether or not to step through the empty place of an unmet need and to embrace opportunities for healing is always yours. Be on the lookout, just in case . . .

In the "Holes and Empty Places" exercise in Chapter Nine you will focus on some of the opportunities for healing that you might encounter when you step through the portals.

Checking In:
My Comfort Level and Feelings

- Where Am I?
- Feelings Gauge
- 21 Ways to Take Care of Myself Right Now

✗ ✎ WHERE AM I?

Place an X on the (1-5) scale below to show your comfort level:

I am extremely <u>uncomfortable</u> exploring who I have been.

I am extremely <u>comfortable</u> exploring who I have been.

1_____2_____3_____4_____5

I put my X very close to :

☐ **5 or 4:** Continue to explore your history and the experiences and beliefs that influenced who you are becoming. With trusted guidance and support (preferably professional), identify any "missing pieces" in your development, along with unfulfilled childhood interests or dreams.

☐ **3:** Pay attention to the parts of your past that you are most comfortable with. Identify positive ways to allow memories of them into your life today. For example: Recall some of your very favorite childhood pastimes and ask, "Why did I love them so much?" Next, notice the parts of your past that are uncomfortable for you to think about. Use writing, the arts, and professional support to help you understand and heal these parts.

☐ **2 or 1:** You may want to seek professional support to: **a)** sort out and clarify what was missing or not a good fit for you in your past **b)** heal "stuffed" emotional pain and/or **c)** define and address fears and conflicts.

Look over the recommendations next to your choice of comfort level (**5 or 4, 3, 2 or 1**). Circle a recommendation you would like to follow through on.

Make a note of it in your notebook or the Back Pocket for future reference. When will you follow through?

What Are You Feeling—*In This Moment?*

Pause, now. Notice the sensations or "messages" your body is giving to you *in this moment.* Do a quick body scan: Begin at the top of your head. Notice your scalp, eyes, and jaw area. Is there tightness anywhere? Notice your shoulders: Are they pulled forward, or are they relaxed and down? Scan your torso, each arm and hand, and both legs and feet. Is there tension anywhere?

If you notice any tension or discomfort, such as tightness, pain, or churning, where is it in your body? Be sure to notice, also, which part of your body is most relaxed. Just notice . . . and breathe.

Use the Feelings Gauge below to help you zero in on your feelings *in this moment.*

FEELINGS GAUGE: WHAT AM I FEELING, *RIGHT NOW?* ©

Circle the number on the scale below that best describes how you are feeling *right now, in this very moment.* **0** represents the calmest feeling state and **10** represents the most upset feeling state. Descriptions of associated body sensations are shown at each extreme to help you gauge where your feelings are *in this moment.*

0 . . .1 . . .2 . . .3 . . .4 . . .5 . . .6 . . .7 . . .8 . . .9 . . .10

Clear	Confused
Centered	Scattered
Relaxed, Still	Tense, Agitated
Nonjudgmental	Reactive, Critical
Slow deep breathing	Rapid breathing
Resting pulse rate	Fast pulse
In total peace	On high alert

NOTE: If you experience feelings of distress while engaged in a Midlife Check-In exercise, these feelings may be a signal to you that it is time to take a break and relax. Symptoms of distress may include one or more of the following: sweaty palms, tension building in your chest, throat tightening, jaw clenching, breathing on hold, nausea, tears, urge to scream or yell, head aching.

Use the following list, "21 Ways to Take Care of Myself Right Now," for suggestions of specific ways to calm yourself in the moment. If painful feelings like these are hard for you to manage in healthy ways, consider seeking professional support.

❖

21 WAYS I CAN TAKE CARE OF MYSELF *RIGHT NOW*

It is important to have simple and effective ways to manage your tension and uncomfortable feelings in the moment. Below are 21 ideas for doing so. Using these can help you move quickly toward a more relaxed and balanced state of being.

☑ Check the ones you like most:

☐ Breathe deeply and slowly

☐ Move freely to music

☐ Stand, stretch, walk around

☐ Do 10-20 jumping jacks

☐ Bend gently side to side, then forward slightly

☐ Beat a drum

☐ Light a candle and be with its light for a few minutes

☐ Hold or stroke my pet

☐ Move to a different space

☐ Watch a funny movie

☐ Climb into my midlife tree

☐ Be in nature near flowers, trees, water, soothing views

☐ Hug myself and breathe

☐ Ring my singing bowl

☐ Speak with a trusted friend

☐ Drink a warm beverage such as herbal tea, milk, soup

☐ Laugh out loud

☐ Shift my body position and breathe deeply

☐ Place my hands over my heart

☐ Focus on an inspiring image

☐ Make a positive statement about myself

Midlife Glossary:
Check Out These Words

Below is a list of glossary words you may wish to explore in relation to this chapter. ☑ Put a check by any that "call" to you, and find their meanings in the Midlife Glossary. How might the words relate to *who you have been*?

☐ assumption	☐ inner child
☐ attachment	☐ magical thinking
☐ awareness	☐ manipulation
☐ catharsis	☐ persona
☐ ego	☐ perspective
☐ emotional needs	☐ regression
☐ empty places	☐ repression
☐ golden nuggets	☐ symbol
☐ heroic thinking	☐ turning point

Sitting Under My Midlife Tree

"If you don't know what to do, sit quietly until your wits come back."
Robert A. Johnson

- Sit and Reflect
- Back Pocket

What captured my attention most?
What puzzled or concerned me?
What do I want to explore further?
How can who I am really affect my life today?

Sit and Reflect

Take a few moments now to climb down from your personal tree of midlife to sit under it and reflect on the question, "Who have I been?" When you are seated in a comfortable spot, take a relaxation belly breath, and let it out slowly.

Open to a few quiet moments with yourself, with no expectations. Consider the work you have done in this chapter "Who Have I Been?" and ask yourself the four questions listed above.

In this space of conversation with yourself insights may grab your attention, questions may surface, or ideas for personal actions may materialize. Who knows? Just relax for a few minutes in your own company as you lean against your midlife tree under its canopy of gently moving leaves. Be . . . and breathe.

Back Pocket

Turn to the Back Pocket or your personal notebook and jot down thoughts, questions, or insights that may have moved through you. How might the symbol you chose earlier reflect them?

You may wish to use one or more of the following ways to give "voice" to your reflections about who you have been: music, drawing, collage, painting, expressive movement, poetry or other writing. Which one calls to you?

Are You Aware That . . . .

. . . . .you may never know what truly happened in your past because it is continually shifting in your memory? At each phase of your life, your past rearranges itself to fit your new sense of yourself and the world.

Chapter Nine

"Who Am I Now?"

> *"Fabulous indeed, amazing for certain, that you are you and I am me."*
> Antonio Damasio

"Who am I *now*?" This question is similar to the one we asked in adolescence and, again, in young adulthood. We asked, "Who am I?" while looking around and comparing ourselves to members of our family, our peer group and others, as well as images in the media.

In our younger years, seeing ourselves in relation to others helped us develop a provisional identity, sometimes called a "false self." Sometimes, we created more than one of these selves, hoping that other people would believe this was who we were. *We* wanted to believe it, too!

In our middle years, we begin to notice that what seemed very important to us in earlier years begins to lose its luster; we no longer resonate with it as strongly, if at all. We <u>wonder</u>, "Why do I feel as if something is missing?" "Is there more to me and my life than meets my eye?"

At this point, we revise the original question. Instead of asking "Who *am* I?", we ask: "Who am I—*now*?" Something has begun whispering to us that, maybe—just maybe—the person we have been showing to the world and thinking we were in past years is not who we can believe we are now. While changes and letting go require more of our attention, our true nature is whispering, "I need you."

To capture or get close to who you are now, as you work in this chapter, you will need to "be here now." You will need to be *with* your experiences and just let them unfold. Take a mindful walk through the open space of the question, who am I now? Be open to what wants to "stir" in you. Being present, in this way, opens and increases your self-awareness, your consciousness.

I recommend that you take a few minutes, at the conclusion of this chapter, to lean against your personal Tree of Midlife and reflect on "Who am I now?" <u>Consider:</u> *What captures my attention most? What puzzles or concerns me? What do I want to explore further? How does who I am now affect my sense of the future?* Notice what colors and patterns your Threads of Becoming are weaving into who you are now.

Record the thoughts, questions, and insights that come to you, about who you are now, in the Back Pocket or your personal notebook. Your time of reflection, while leaning against the tree, may give you your most valuable information about who you are now.

In this chapter, you will increase your understanding of who you are now. You will:

- Focus on the positives,
- Explore your present identity, and
- Dig Deeper.

You will also use the "Where Am I?" and the "Feeling Gauge" exercises to check in with your comfort level and your feelings.

You can extend your knowledge and deepen your understanding of midlife by exploring "Midlife Glossary: Check Out These Words." Find their meanings in the Midlife Glossary.

ɤ **NOTE:** *If, at any time, while engaging in this chapter, you do not feel comfortable with what comes up, turn to "21 Ways to Take Care of Myself Right Now" on page 117 and follow the directions. Take a break. Check in with a professional, if your discomfort continues and interferes with your daily functioning.*

Focusing on the Positives

• My Golden Nuggets: Hidden Assets
• My Story: Rescripting a Challenging Experience

MY GOLDEN NUGGETS:
Hidden Assets

In Chapter Seven, you identified golden nuggets, from your pre-midlife years. Drawing on these valuable assets in midlife can strengthen your sense of self and your confidence. Review what you wrote on your list of golden nuggets. In addition to other things, your list may include: skills you learned, goals you worked for, courage you drew upon, compassion you developed, and/or lessons learned.

A specific skill, a lesson learned, or your ability to be compassionate can help you "de-fuse" the hot spots in your life. Your courage, your skill in setting clear boundaries, or your ability to take healthy risks can help you bring new and positive energy into your life.

When you draw upon your golden nuggets to help you in the present, you are investing in the future. Drawing on your personal nuggets can help you improve situations, increase hope, build inner strength, and open yourself and others to new possibilities. Have you used any golden nuggets recently?

Consider a current challenge in your life. Is there some part of this situation that is hard for you to manage, or that you cannot seem to resolve? Select one or two of your nuggets that could help you manage the difficulty you are facing.

Challenge: _____

Nugget: How I Might Use It:

1._____   _____

2._____   _____

MY STORY:
Rescripting a Challenging Experience

It is not uncommon for life to offer us challenges similar to ones we have faced before. While the names and places that are involved may change, difficult circumstances are bound to play a role in our life. Ideally, when this happens, we will draw on what we learned from our earlier experience (golden nuggets!) to meet and manage the challenge with more skill.

Recall an event or situation that was a challenge for you to handle sometime during the last three to four years. For example, you might have had to "draw the line" or change the rules in an important relationship. Maybe you had to resolve a deep ambivalence about something you knew, deep down, would shift your life for the better. Perhaps your challenge centered on an unexpected and significant loss.

Whatever your personal example of a difficult situation may be, here is the question: "If you had the chance to do it over, to meet this same challenge again, how might you handle it differently?" What might you do to put a more positive spin on this experience? How would you "rescript" it?

> ✍ **NOTE:** *The following exercise may be one you will want to work on with a therapist. Processing your hindsight with professional support can help you: 1) deepen your understanding of what made the experience challenging for you, and 2) learn appropriate ways to improve similar situations in the future.*

Rescripting Your Past Challenge

In this exercise, you are going to rescript the original version of a challenging experience you had in recent years. You will think ahead to how you might handle a similar situation, in the future, with greater confidence and, perhaps, less regret. Your hindsight and insight will help you do this.

To recreate your previous experience in a more positive light, change one or more aspects of the parts *you* played in it—any that you believe could make it more positive. The parts might include what you did to bring about the experience, how you responded (or *reacted*) to it, and the way you left it.

Aspects of the parts you played that you might want to change include: your attitude, assumptions you made, and specific things you did. You can change your specific actions, your words, and even your body language.

My Challenge, Rescripted

Name of the Challenge: _____

Reason(s) for Making Changes in This Experience:

_____

_____

_____

_____

Part(s) I Want to Rescript

☑ Check the part(s) you plan to change:
   ☐ What I did to bring about this challenging experience
   ☐ How I responded or reacted to the experience
   ☐ The way I left the experience/the ending

➔ What I would do differently:

_____

_____

_____

Aspects I Am Rescripting

☑ Check the one(s) you plan to change:
   ☐ My attitude
   ☐ An assumption I made
   ☐ Specific behaviors/things I did, said, or gestured

➔ What I would change about this aspect:

_____

_____

_____

Exploring My Identity

- Baby Boomer or Generation X-er?
  - My Identity in the Present
    - What Brings Me Joy?
  - A Symbol of Who I Am Now

BABY BOOMER OR GENERATION X-ER?

You cannot escape the role and power that history has had in shaping who you are. The traits and beliefs you may have assumed as a member of the generation you grew up in influence your sense of who you are and what matters to you.

Are you a Golden Boomer? A Baby Boomer? Or a Generation X-er? In this exercise, you will explore the distinguishing traits, beliefs, and events of your generation. Which of these do you resonate with most? Some items may be ones you have long forgotten!

The cutoff year of 1946 for Golden Boomers is based on population statistics of the post-war years. Needless to say, if you were born just three or four years earlier, you will have had many of the experiences listed in the first section.

Golden Boomer

☐ I was born between 1946 and 1955.

☐ My peers and I were more likely to "stick it out" at work, even if we were unhappy.

☐ Desires of a husband, boss, or son matter more than a woman's.

☐ Martin Luther King was assassinated when I was in my 20s.

☐ I had Slinky, the *new* toy, when I was a child.

☐ Drug experimentation (LSD, etc.) developed in my generation.

☐ My generation is typically uncomfortable with discussions about aging and planning for end-of-life.

☐ I am getting close to retirement age.

☐ Words I might use to describe my generation in its *younger* years, the 60s and 70s, are free-spirited, anti-war, sexually free, oriented toward social causes (women's movement, civil rights, the environment, gay rights, handicapped rights).

☐ *Rock and Roll* was popular when I was a teenager.

☐ I watched or listened to the landing on the moon by American astronauts.

☐ My family had a transistor radio when I was a young teenager.

☐ JFK was assassinated when I was in high school or college.

☐ Around 1985-1990, I was *becoming* middle-aged.

☐ When "9-11" occurred, I was in my late 40s or in my 50s.

Baby Boomer

☐ I was born between 1956 and 1964.

☐ Working on my career has been the main focus in my life during the last 25 years.

☐ I am pondering, "What is my life about? What does the women's movement mean?"

☐ Most of my life I have felt optimistic about opportunities to succeed.

☐ I have been accustomed to receiving an Employee Benefits Package.

☐ Barbie Dolls first became popular when I was a child.

☐ The question "how do you have it all" is on my mind.

☐ JFK was assassinated when I was in elementary school.

☐ Over the years, I have acquired 10-25 years of on-the-job experience.

☐ When I was in high school or college, President Nixon resigned, there were gasoline shortages in the US, and Punk or *New Wave* music was becoming popular.

☐ Earning money and being recognized for my work has felt good.

☐ I'm having to learn new tools that replace my old ones in order to stay competitive in my job, career, or business.

☐ I was almost a teen in 1974.

☐ Expectations of women, gays, and marriage are shifting from those of the previous generation.

☐ My generation tends to focus on the values of youthful appearance and lifestyle, and who we spend time with.

☐ Shopping at K-MART or WAL-MART was new when I was young.

☐ The Vietnam War ended when I was in my teens.

☐ Words or phrases I might use to describe my generation in its earlier years include reactive, amoral, negative, focused on $, diverse life styles, seeking leisure time with peace of mind.

☐ I was, or know someone in my age bracket who was, involved in the Vietnam War.

☐ Financial planning is increasingly important to me

☐ Many of my job skills are becoming outdated or less efficient.

☐ While I was growing up, I expected that the world would improve with time; the future would get better and better.

☐ I'm most comfortable knowing what I was trained for and drawing on my expertise in that field.

☐ I prefer documented feedback for my annual review at work.

☐ My generation does not take "no" for an answer. We want to keep going and going and, by God, we will!!

Generation X-er

☐ I was born between 1965 and 1981.

☐ My peers and I have been willing to pick up and leave a job that is not satisfying.

☐ Women hold responsible positions in the workplace more and more frequently.

☐ My peers typically slept with their partner before being married.

☐ I multi-task naturally to keep up and stay connected in the world.

☐ Changes in job and career are part of life. They help me build knowledge and increase my skills and keep me engaged.

☐ Having friends and co-workers whose parents are divorced is not unusual.

☐ Being loyal to one company or major employer doesn't make much sense anymore.

☐ I want to feel that I'm living a balanced life.

☐ *Heavy Metal and Hip-Hop* culture music came into being.

☐ I have grown up with a sense of an uncertain, ill-defined future, especially economically and politically.

☐ I prefer having a flexible work schedule with options to help me juggle family and work.

☐ Paying attention to the foods and life style that help me have a healthy mind and body is an idea I like.

☐ I have used computers and the internet nearly all of my adult life.

☐ I want a career that is "portable."

<u>While you were going through the list for your generation, did you think of other items not listed?</u>

Did You Know?

An interesting fact about the midlife experience is that someone can be a Baby Boomer and be feeling and thinking like someone who is in the psychological shifts of Phase 3 in midlife. At the same time, someone can be a Golden Boomer, in her late sixties, and be experiencing psychological shifts typical of Phase 2 of midlife. We ebb and flow . . . .

MY IDENTITY IN THE PRESENT

In the previous exercise you took a look at who you are now from the finite context of history. You explored its outside influences on your life. Now you are going to look at who you are from a non-finite context—the fluid, complex, and changeable place of your inner world.

The following exercise zeros in on your current hopes, dreams, ideals, goals, voice, roles, and self-expectations.

• Images or models that help me to define myself today:

_____

_____

_____

• Hopes, dreams, or ideals I aspire to:

_____

_____

_____

• Personal goals I have now:

_____

_____

_____

• My voice and how I use it most of the time (e.g. agreeing, speaking out, writing, making news, whining, collaborating, partnering, persuading, helping others, making decisions independently, giving in to others, rebelling, consenting, performing, etc.):

_____

_____

_____

The message(s) I most want others to "get":

_____

_____

_____

• The primary roles I play in my life (student, parent, partner, spouse, loyal friend, child, lover, leader, caregiver, loner, rebellious daughter, dutiful daughter, active healer, member of community organizations, peacemaker, etc.):

_____

_____

_____

• 3 important people in my life who have a major impact on who I am now (family members, friends, teachers, mentors, co-workers, spouses, lovers, etc.) are:

_____

_____

_____

• Expectations I have for myself include

_____

_____

_____

Are these expectations yours or someone else's?

• The persona I am living now is one I (circle one) *want/ don't want* to keep. The parts of my persona that I plan to keep include:

_____

_____

_____

Changes I would like to make in my persona include:

_____

_____

_____

WHAT BRINGS ME JOY?

The feeling of joy is an essential part of living who you truly are. Moments of joy can sustain you during challenging times. When you feel joy, you shift your brain and body chemistries; you shift your mood to one that is healing. Consider these examples of what can generate joy in us:

- Biting into a crisp, juicy apple
- The pleasure of a well-told story
- Stopping to get a cup of coffee
- Admiring blossoms on a cherry tree
- The relish of a well-chosen word
- The familiarity of treasured people and places
- Tasting a favorite food
- Anticipating a reunion with someone special
- Staring out the window and marveling at the unique and beautiful cloud formations
- Being held tenderly by someone you love
- Seeing someone's face light up with joy

What brings you joy and how your body expresses it are special parts of who you are. What brings *you* joy? How does *your* body experience moments of joy? Name some of these experiences and thoughts below:

_____

_____

_____

A SYMBOL OF WHO I AM NOW

While working with the focus question in this chapter, feelings, beliefs, energy, and/or values about who you are now may have emerged in you. What inner sense do you have of yourself? What symbol that you know (or might create) could represent the deeper meaning or sense *you* have of who you are now?

If nothing comes to mind, look around your environments for objects and ideas. Browse magazines and online image collections. Look at designs on book covers. Look at images in nature. What jumps out at you? What may hold some or all of the meaning of who you are now?

Choose something. Make a note or put the image in the Back Pocket or in your personal notebook. In the last part of the book, Part Four, you will bring together this symbol, the one from the previous chapter, and one more you will identify in the next chapter.

Digging Deeper

- Ten Below
- Notice and Reflect
- Holes and Empty Places: Portals to Opportunity

TEN BELOW

The 10 statements below can help you dig deeper and respond to the question, "Who am I now?" They might help you connect with aspects of yourself and your present way of life that you may or may not have thought about recently.

As you read each statement, be spontaneous; fill in what comes to mind first. If you cannot think of something to write, go on to the remaining items and come back. The best approach is to work from your gut. The best policy is honesty. Remember: this is for YOU!

☐ **1.** What I absolutely *love* about myself is

_____

_____

☐ **2.** I get "fired up" with excitement when

_____

_____

☐ **3.** I use my authentic or "true" voice (the one that comes from a deeper place in me) most easily and comfortably when

_____

_____

☐ **4.** For me, love and intimacy are

_____

_____

☐ **5.** At this time in my life, I am determined to achieve

_____

_____.

☐ **6.** An inspiring piece of wisdom that is very helpful to me in life is

_____

_____.

☐ **7.** An obstacle or "hard place" in my life that I am learning to deal with is

_____

_____.

☐ **8.** Something about myself that I would like to change or to overcome is

_____

_____.

☐ **9.** _____

_____

greatly influences how I feel about myself as a person.

☐ **10.** A part of myself that I keep hidden from others is

_____

_____.

✍ NOTICE and REFLECT
Review the 10 statements you completed above:

Notice:

- Which statements were easy for you to answer?
- Which statements were especially difficult for you to answer?
  ☑Put a check next to them.

✍ **NOTE:** *A strong, uncomfortable reaction to completing a statement may suggest that something in you cries out for mending; there may be "unfinished business" that needs healing resolution. If so, seeking professional support may be appropriate for you.*

Reflect:

- Do any concerns or issues call out to you to be resolved? If you are in the habit of keeping a journal, working with the arts, having a meditation practice or other quiet time, consider using one of the statements you checked as a focus for reflection.

✍Jot down what you notice about your responses:

_____

_____

_____

HOLES AND EMPTY PLACES:
Portals to Opportunity

✎ **NOTE:** *If you are currently dealing with a personal crisis or another emotional upheaval, please consider working on the following exercise in partnership with a licensed therapist. Or, come back to this when you feel grounded.*

In "Holes and Empty Places from My Past" in Chapter Eight, you considered any empty places that may have been left in you, early on, by unmet emotional needs. You also looked at any unhealthy strategies you may have been (or are) using to get these needs met. Each empty place, or "hole," that remains inside of you is a part of who you are.

Our basic emotional needs include:

- feeling loved
- feeling we belong
- feeling safe
- feeling worthy

In this exercise, you will consider how stepping *through* empty places can begin to heal them. In Chapter Ten you will consider the empty places you want to move through and heal.

Awareness Is the Key

When we become aware of an unmet emotional need and any unhealthy strategies we have been using to meet that need, we are close to stepping through the opening or portal into healthy opportunities to heal. We are standing at the threshold.

As our awareness increases, so may our readiness to heal. When we are conscious of our unmet need(s) and we *want* to heal, we have a greater chance of doing so. Our awareness and willingness prepare us for healing our emotional wounds, strengthening our sense of self-worth, and deepening our compassion for self and others.

<u>Opportunities for Healing—in Disguise</u>

We may not recognize opportunities for personal growth and healing at first glance; they may show up in disguise. For example, an opportunity to begin healing a fear, or the empty place of not feeling safe, is showing up when a situation challenges us to face one of our fears.

Perhaps we fear speaking up—on the job, with our partner, in the doctor's office. We may have learned, early on, that our honest expression of feelings or opinions was not ok; when we spoke up, we were punished or told to "be quiet." Consequently, feeling unsafe to be our true Self developed into an empty place. We learned to keep our feelings inside and to withhold expressions of our authentic Self; we became what *others* were comfortable with in us. We played it "safe."

When we step up to the plate, knees quivering and heart racing, and enter into an uncomfortable situation we would normally avoid, we are beginning to heal an empty place. We have recognized a healthy opportunity to grow and to heal disguised in this situation, and we are about to seize it!

When someone with low self-confidence turns to you for help you may have an opportunity to begin healing your own low sense of self-worth and belonging. Healing often occurs when we extend our self to others and we help them meet the very need that was not met in us.

Another healing opportunity in disguise may be a person who wants to reconcile differences with you. Or it may be your own desire to free yourself from the bonds of resentment. Your decision to let go of anger and make amends to someone has the power to heal an empty place created by experiences of feeling rejected. Being proactive in this healthy way can shift you out of the victim stance and into healing mode.

When we accept a challenge to overcome a fear that has held us back, when we extend our self to others, and when we make amends to others we are using healthy strategies to help us heal our unmet needs. In the process, we are strengthening our sense of self-worth and deepening our compassion for self and for others.

You will discover opportunities to heal and to strengthen your character and compassion by being on alert for them. The choice of whether or not to step through the empty place of an unmet need is always yours. Be on the lookout, just in case . . .

Have you sighted any opportunities for healing and personal growth lately?

Opportunity:_____

Opportunity:_____

Opportunity:_____

❖

Checking In:
My Comfort Level and Feelings

- Where Am I?
- Feelings Gauge
- 21 Ways to Take Care of Myself Right Now

✗✎ WHERE AM I?

Place an X on the (1-5) scale below to show your comfort level:

*I am extremely <u>uncomfortable</u>
living in my midlife skin.*

*I am extremely <u>comfortable</u>
living in my midlife skin.*

1_____2_____3_____4_____5

I put my X very close to :

☐ **5 or 4:** Continue focusing on what is working well for you in your life. Explore new ways to express "you" out in the world. Choose something to learn or to become better at. Set a personal goal and go for it!

☐ **3:** Keep growing the parts of yourself you are most comfortable with. Take inventory of the parts that feel uncomfortable. Choose one; practice building personal comfort and ease with this part.

☐ **2 or 1:** You may want to seek professional support to: **a)** clarify what is missing, painful, or not a good fit for you in your life; **b)** heal current and past emotional pain; and/or **c)** connect with the "real" you.

Look over the recommendations next to your choice of comfort level (**5 or 4, 3, 2 or 1**). Circle a recommendation you would like to follow through on.

Make a note of this in your Back Pocket or personal notebook for future reference. When will you follow through?

What Are You Feeling—*In This Moment?*

Pause, now. Notice the sensations or "messages" your body is giving to you *in this moment.* Do a quick body scan: Begin at the top of your head. Notice your scalp, eyes, and jaw area. Is there tightness anywhere? Notice your shoulders: Are they pulled forward, or are they relaxed and down? Scan your torso, each arm and hand, and both legs and feet. Is there tension anywhere?

If you notice any tension or discomfort, such as tightness, pain, or churning, where is it in your body? Be sure to notice, also, which part of your body is most relaxed. Just notice . . . and breathe.

Use the Feelings Gauge below to help you zero in on your feelings *in this moment.*

FEELINGS GAUGE:
WHAT AM I FEELING, *RIGHT NOW?*

Circle the number on the scale below that best describes how you are feeling *right now, in this very moment.* **0** represents the calmest feeling state and **10** represents the most upset feeling state. Descriptions of associated body sensations are shown at each extreme to help you gauge where your feelings are *in this moment.*

0 . . .1 . . .2 . . .3 . . .4 . . .5 . . .6 . . .7 . . .8 . . .9 . . .10

Clear..Confused
Centered...Scattered
Relaxed, Still ....Tense, Agitated
Nonjudgmental ....Reactive, Critical
Slow deep breathing ....Rapid breathing
Resting pulse rate..Fast pulse
In total peace...On high alert

NOTE: If you experience feelings of distress while engaged in a Midlife Check-In exercise, these feelings may be a signal to you that it is time to take a break and relax. Symptoms of distress may include one or more of the following: sweaty palms, tension building in your chest, throat tightening, jaw clenching, breathing on hold, nausea, tears, urge to scream or yell, head aching.

Use the following list, "21 Ways to Take Care of Myself Right Now," for suggestions of specific ways to calm yourself in the moment. If painful feelings like these are hard for you to manage in healthy ways, consider seeking professional support.

❖

21 WAYS I CAN TAKE CARE OF MYSELF
RIGHT NOW

It is important to have simple and effective ways to manage your tension and uncomfortable feelings in the moment. Below are 21 ideas for doing so. Using these can help you move quickly toward a more relaxed and balanced state of being.

☑ Check the ones you like most:

☐ Breathe deeply and slowly

☐ Move freely to music

☐ Stand, stretch, walk around

☐ Do 10-20 jumping jacks

☐ Bend gently side to side, then forward slightly

☐ Beat a drum

☐ Light a candle and be with its light for a few minutes

☐ Hold or stroke my pet

☐ Move to a different space

☐ Watch a funny movie

☐ Climb into my midlife tree

☐ Be in nature near flowers, trees, water, soothing views

☐ Hug myself and breathe

☐ Ring my singing bowl

☐ Speak with a trusted friend

☐ Drink a warm beverage such as herbal tea, milk, soup

☐ Laugh out loud

☐ Shift my body position and breathe deeply

☐ Place my hands over my heart

☐ Focus on an inspiring image

☐ Make a positive statement about myself

**Midlife Glossary:
Check Out These Words**

Below is a list of glossary words you may wish to explore in relation to this chapter. ☑ Put a check by any words that "call" to you, and find their meanings in the Midlife Glossary. How might the words relate to *who you are now*?

☐ archetype/archetypal energy

☐ boundaries

☐ containers

☐ human thinking

☐ identity

☐ intimacy

☐ self-concept

☐ shifts

☐ wounded inner child

Leaning Against My Midlife Tree

"What is it that stands higher than words? Action.
What is it that stands higher than action? Silence."
Francis of Assisi

- Lean Back and Reflect
- Back Pocket

What captures my attention most?
What puzzles or concerns me?
What do I want to explore further?
How does who I am now influence my sense of the future?

Lean Back and Reflect

Take a few moments now to climb down from your personal tree of midlife to lean against it and reflect on the question, "Who am I now?" When you feel comfortably supported by your tree, take a relaxation belly breath, and let it out slowly.

Open to a few quiet moments with yourself, with no expectations. Consider the work you have done in this chapter "Who Am I Now?" and ask yourself the four questions listed above.

In this space of conversation with yourself insights may grab your attention, questions may surface, or ideas for personal action may materialize. Who knows? Just relax for a few minutes in your own company in the nurturing shelter of your midlife tree. Be . . . and breathe.

Back Pocket

Turn to the Back Pocket or your personal notebook and jot down thoughts, questions, or insights that may have moved through you. How might the symbols you chose earlier reflect them?

You may wish to use one or more of the following ways to give "voice" to your reflections about who you are now. Which one calls to you: music, drawing, collage, painting, expressive movement, poetry or other writing?

The Value of Your Check-In Process, So Far

The goal of this and the previous chapters has been to focus on aspects of yourself that you are aware of or can recall. Some of these aspects include your generation, past experiences, skills and abilities, relationships, roles, goals, interests, comfort level, and feelings. Self-perceptions concerning these characteristics and others make up a collection of beliefs you have about yourself. We call this your "self-concept."

The gender stereotypes we grew up with; our parents' expectations for us; and the feedback we receive from peers, teachers, colleagues, bosses, partners, and family members have an impact on our understanding of who we have been and are now. As we interpret our feelings and our abilities and performance, we are in the process of developing our self-concept.

Perspective

Your self-concept changes as you reassess who you are at various stages and points in your life. Your responses to the Midlife Check-In exercises, if given ten years ago or ten years from now, would be different from the ones you are giving today. Consider this.

All of your responses are important. They serve as a mirror reflecting your past and present choices, decisions, and beliefs. Making honest responses to the exercises helps you notice how you have lived and are living your life. It connects you with information and parts of yourself that you may seldom, if ever, consider.

The information you have given will also help you to make important choices, in Chapter Ten, about who and how you want to become now and in the coming years. You have gathered all of this information, so far, through the eyes of your ego or personality—that is to say, your conscious self. The next chapter will show you how to gather information from a very different place in yourself—your unconscious.

Chapter Ten

Who Am I *Really*?
A Blend of the Seen and the Unseen

> *"Walking along*
> *My shadow beside me*
> *Watching the moon."*
> SODŌ

"Who am I *really*?" To explore this question we will enter new and fascinating territory in your Midlife Check-In process. In previous chapters you gathered information about yourself by using ordinary self-awareness, also called "conscious perspective," or ego. You used direct observation and memory to capture and record what you can see and recall easily about yourself. What you will discover in Chapter Ten is that what you have gathered, so far, is not the entire picture . . .

While that information is very important, it is only the small, "seen" part of who you are *really*. The majority of who you are actually lives *beneath* your everyday thinking or conscious perspective; it is "unseen." We refer to this place as your unconscious.

Your sense of who you are, when based only on what your ego sees, is a very narrow or limited view; it is like trying to view a panorama of the Grand Canyon or the Atlantic Ocean using a telescope! The large majority of what is actually there is left out. Who you really are is made up of the entire panorama plus even more that you may never see.

<u>Stepping Out for a Larger View</u>

This chapter will help you to step out of your ego's limited self-perception and connect with some of the more elusive elements of who you are in your unconscious. You will, however, have to *sense* them if you are going to connect with them. No doubt, you have experience doing so. For example, you may have:

- had a gut feeling
- felt unexpected attraction to or disgust for something
- experienced a flash of insight or an "Aha!" moment
- spoken words that did not seem to be yours
- recalled a dream

<u>Gathering More Insights</u>

Engaging with the exercises in this chapter can enlarge your sense of the seen and unseen elements in you and deepen your awareness of who you are *really*. What you discover in this introductory experience will be a valuable addition to your earlier insights about who you have been and who you are now. When you feel your depths, you create an inner "home," a more felt sense of Self. Attending to the visible and not-so-visible parts of yourself can be transformative.

I recommend that, after you have completed the exercises in this chapter, you take a few minutes to sit under or lean against your midlife tree and reflect on who you are *really*. What colors and patterns might your Threads of Becoming be weaving at a deeper level inside of you?

I have found, in my experience, that relaxed and thoughtful reflection is the source of my most valuable and useful insights about myself, my life, and creative projects. While leaning against your midlife tree, you may find this to be true for you, as well.

What comes into your awareness may shed light on or deepen your sense of the seen and unseen aspects of who you really are. Record your thoughts, questions, and insights in the Back Pocket or in your personal notebook.

Your Mental Broom

As you work in this chapter, pay close attention to negative self-talk and any judgments, criticisms, or "shoulds" that your ego recites to you! It is only trying to distract you and dissuade you from connecting with the larger sense of who you are because it feels threatened or afraid. It is defending its narrower view. When you encounter these negative distractions, tell your ego "not now" and use your mental broom to SSWWWISH them away.

In this chapter, you will enlarge and deepen your understanding of Who you are really. You will:

- Get grounded in new territory
- Focus on the positives
- Explore your identity
- Dig deeper.

You will also check in with your feelings, using the "Feelings Gauge" exercise.

You may wish to extend your knowledge and deepen your understanding of midlife by exploring "Midlife Glossary: Check Out These Words." Find their meanings in the Midlife Glossary.

⊘ NOTE: *If, at any time, while engaging in this chapter, you do not feel comfortable with what comes up, turn to "21 Ways to Take Care of Myself Right Now" on page 172 and follow the directions. Take a break. Check in with a professional, if your discomfort continues and interferes with your daily functioning.*

Getting Grounded

1. Wholeness = Self
2. Integration: Our Process of Becoming Whole
3. The "Not-Knowing"

First Step:

An important first step into new territory is getting grounded. The three parts of "Getting Grounded" will give you the basics about the seen and unseen parts of who you are.

Reading these parts and responding candidly to the exercises about your "real" self will help anchor you before going on to the exercises in the rest of this chapter.

1. WHOLENESS = SELF: Your Conscious Perspective

• Your Unconscious
• The "You" Behind Your Eyes
• The Relationship Between Seen and Unseen

From my life experience, my creative work, the literature I have read, and my work as a therapist and educator, I have come to believe there is a vital force within us that continually nudges and guides us toward our inherent wholeness, our true Self. It is a current that runs through us but does not seem to belong to us. This core energy is like the shoot of life hidden within the core of a tulip bulb that, over its lifetime, directs the plant to produce a beautiful flower.

I will use the sphere, shown in the next part, to illustrate the ideas of "wholeness" and "Self." The sphere contains three core elements: 1) what you are conscious of in your day-to-day life, 2) what exists outside of your consciousness that, typically, you are not aware of, and 3) the connections that can develop between them. Together, these three elements make up your "whole" or complete Self, the one we spell with a capital "S." In psychology, we use the word "psyche" to name this totality of who we are. When we feel "whole," we have a sense of inner order—a sense that, within us, all is well.

A wonderful image of the Self is your own handprint made in the sand, wet cement, or in paint. Do you recall pressing your hand into one of these as a child? To *become* "whole" requires inner work. It is a conscious choice to look at and heal what is holding you back and limiting the growth of Self. Inner work deepens your Self-awareness and promotes your emotional wellness. It generates a space of newness in yourself, a space for growing into wholeness.

Your Conscious Perspective: What Your Ego Sees and Thinks

Your ego is made up of protective layers, shaped over time by your upbringing, your generation, and by society's values. Your ego, also called personality, is the most *human* part of who you are, the part that needs to feel safe. It notices things in your environment that may threaten your physical and emotional safety. It is the part of you that needs to feel it is loved and worthy and that it belongs. Your ego is the source of self-consciousness. When we ask, "Am I doing this right? What will they think? Do I look ok?" and so on, we are expressing self-consciousness. Because your ego's agenda is *survival*, it typically responds with fear or control to what feels threatening or with an unhealthy attachment to someone. Sometimes your ego may feel challenged when you make choices it does not want you to make. It may push your deeper needs and feelings to the side so that you will fit in with others and feel "safe." Because these reactions are so habitual, you can come to believe, mistakenly, that the ego is who you really are. To move beyond this narrow belief and into your unique potential, you must explore and understand what the ego does not want you to see.

Your ego, or personality, is self with a small "s." It is your conscious perspective and it includes, among other things, your thoughts, plans, goals, likes and dislikes, awareness of what goes on in your physical environment, and memories. While your ego is actually a very minor part of who you are, it is the part you are most aware of; it consumes the greater part of your attention.

Your Unconscious: What Your Ego Does Not Want You to See

Living and moving in a deeper place beneath the veil of your ego-self is your unconscious. It is the majority of who you are really. The forest in Dante's *Divine Comedy* is an often-cited metaphor for the unconscious.

The kinds of things moving around in this deeper place include: hidden motivations; repressed desires; intuitive and gut feelings; your inherent drive to create; parts of yourself you have cut off or denied; dreams, symbols, and images you may or may not remember when you awaken; ways you defend yourself against fear; sudden insights; forgotten emotional wounds; impulses that spring up in you unexpectedly; and positive and negative personal characteristics you have not expressed in the world.

Communicating in Bits and Pieces

At any given time, your unconscious may show you bits and pieces of itself. It does this by generating feelings, images, and symbols to communicate with you. These are usually fleeting glimpses only. If you are not paying attention, these messengers can move through you easily without being noticed or recognized. They can become lost in the daily shuffle of your ego's choices and decisions.

Bits and Pieces That Get Your Attention

More than likely, you have experienced your unconscious in ways you could sense, but could not explain. For example, maybe you have had the experience of noticing something you ordinarily would not "see," like an image or word that grabs your attention without warning? It feels as if it jumped right in front of your line of sight or that something *made* your eyes notice it.

When you remember a dream or parts of it, you are connecting with information from your unconscious. Maybe you have had a feeling inside of you that would not go away; it kept gnawing at you, perhaps distracting and annoying you? Or you have noticed that certain, unwanted feelings come up in you *unexpectedly* and, sometimes, often.

These are all ways your unconscious works to get your attention—and always with good reason. It is nudging you, ultimately, to become more *Self* conscious (vs. self-conscious) and to grow toward wholeness.

Out of the Blue

As you work with this chapter, be alert for what may come into your awareness from "out of the blue." Take note . . . Write about an experience, paint or dance it, or express it in another way. These kinds of candid, personal expression can expand your self-awareness and deepen your experience. They can give you insight about what may be going on in you at a deeper level. Somatic experiences, in particular, can strengthen the connection between your ego and more authentic Self.

As you pay more attention to the bits and pieces coming from your unconscious, you grow toward wholeness and develop who you are *really*.

❖

THE "YOU" BEHIND YOUR EYES: WHO IS LOOKING BACK AT YOU?

To begin moving closer to the unseen part of yourself, try this simple exercise, "The 'You' Behind Your Eyes."

✗ **Caveat:** Nora Ephron once wrote: *"If I must look into [a mirror], I begin by squinting, so that if anything really bad is looking back at me, I am already halfway to closing my eyes to ward off the sight."* In the following exercise, pay attention that it is *your* eyes you are looking through! Sometimes, we look into our mirror and see our self through someone else's eyes, not our own.

For example, we may be "seeing" what we think our parent or partner might perceive. *"You aren't enough, you need to smile more, you aren't loving, you're passive, you're too fat"* are examples of what we may be "seeing." Sometimes what we see is an imagined "less-than" self.

When that happens, step forward or lean into the mirror and speak back: *"I make my own decisions about who I am and what I want in my life. I am in charge of me, not you."* So, double check the words you hear as you look into your eyes. Is it you or someone else speaking? Are you looking through *your* eyes? Or someone *else's*?

Begin:
1. Go to a wall mirror or use a hand mirror.
2. Relax yourself with a few deep breaths.
3. Look into the mirror at yourself, and focus your attention on your eyes; look only at your eyes.
4. Continue to breathe and relax, while looking at your eyes.
5. Now, look *into* your eyes; *gaze* into them. Imagine that you can see *through* your eyes and *beyond* them.
6. Be aware of any energy or feeling you sense behind your eyes. Notice: What has heart and meaning deep inside of you?
7. Continue for a few moments in this way, noticing the energy or feelings that come into your awareness.
8. Take a deep breath, relax, and come back to focus on yourself and your Midlife Check-In process.

ᦸ **Notice:**

What happened for you as you changed your focus from looking at the outside of your eyes to gazing into and through them?

Did you connect with anything beyond your eyes?

You are so much more than meets the eye—yours and anyone else's.

The Relationship Between Seen (Conscious) and Unseen (Unconscious)

To better understand the relationship of your ego or conscious perspective and the major part of you that functions beneath your awareness, think about an iceberg: typically, just one-ninth of an entire iceberg is visible above the water's surface; the vast majority of the iceberg is deep below the surface, out of sight.

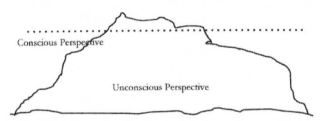

Thus, in any given instant, who we really are is more than we can know. We need all of our psychological processes, the ones we are conscious of and those beneath our awareness, to become "whole," our unique potential, our true Self.

We need the parts of our Self that we like and are conscious of, as well as the parts that are difficult for us to acknowledge or accept. All of our processes and parts make up our unique potential, our whole Self. The more conscious of these we become and the more comfortable we become with acknowledging them in ourselves, the more we move from the self-consciousness of our ego into the Self consciousness of wholeness. The result is greater movement toward our wholeness. As strange as it may seem, making your handprints in sand, cement, or paint, helps you move in this direction.

2. INTEGRATION:
Our Process of Becoming Whole, Our Self

• Traits Associated with Being Real
• My Personal Integration: Where Am I?

As your awareness and acknowledgement of both the conscious and the veiled aspects within you increase and deepen over time, these elements shift and gradually overlap with one other. We call this process "integration." The graphic below illustrates this concept.

Integration of Your Conscious and Unconscious Elements

Split   *Integration Process*   *Wholeness*
(Taking Place Over a Lifetime)

A Container for New Growth

As your conscious and hidden aspects shift and overlap, a shared space develops between them:

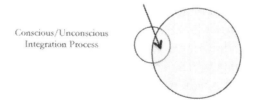

Conscious/Unconscious
Integration Process

This space of overlap is a kind of container or womb in which something new begins to form and germinate in you. It is a place where new life can develop. The shared space between your conscious and the hidden parts of yourself becomes the place of new awareness in you; insights, deep understandings, meaningful inner connections, Self-acceptance, passion, and purpose form and grow in this place.

As your awareness grows and integration is taking place, this space becomes larger to accommodate your increasing consciousness of who you are; the "bud" in you begins to open. Recall: When the tiny shoot of life at the core of the tulip bulb directs the plant toward its wholeness, a new life eventually emerges in the magnificent flower.

What Does Integration Look Like?

At some point in time, you probably have encountered or know someone who feels "real." She draws you in or gets your attention with her presence. It is not about something she is doing; it is her state of being. You get a feeling that she is comfortable with who she is. What you experience in your encounter with her is something simple and unpretentious. It is a "now-ness," the life at her center.

You can feel her genuineness, that she is not using a persona to impress others or to feel safe with you. She feels safe with who she is. She knows what matters most to her at a deeper level, and she behaves in ways that support this. She is able to express and act her courageous and determined self, as well as her softer more nurturing self. She is balanced.

"Centered" might be another word you would use to describe this person. At the very least, this person seems to be able to manage the ups and downs of her life and her emotions without falling apart. None of this is meant to say that she is perfect and flawless. This is, after all, a human being. More consistently than not, however, she "walks her talk." The qualities you sense about her being "real" are reflections of the integration process that is going on within her.

When you meet or know someone who impresses you in these ways, you are very fortunate. This person is modeling for you the best of who you can be. What you admire in *her* is part of your *own* unique potential for inner balance; it is something in *you* that you are not yet aware of or have not yet developed. It is a part of yourself that is unconscious and you are seeing it in someone else.

TRAITS ASSOCIATED WITH BEING "REAL"

The list below offers several of the traits usually associated with people who are in a conscious process of personal integration. No doubt, at various times, you have observed some of these traits in others, *as well as* in yourself. These traits emerge in us as our process of integration evolves and our consciousness increases and deepens.

Take a look at the list. ☑Check the traits you recognize in yourself—even if only from time to time. Be honest; that is part of becoming whole!

___ Focused, clear, centered

___ Compassionate, forgiving

___ Seldom gives "double messages"

___ Usually balances work, lay, rest

___ Confident, strong, purposeful

___ Peaceful, calm

___ Able to delay gratification

___ Realistically optimistic

___ Can discern who to trust with what

___ Assertive in respectful ways

___ Appreciative, grateful

___ Aware, engaged, active

___ Evolving, living a clear life purpose

___ Seeks positive people & settings

___ Usually feeling "up"

___ Usually patient

__ Genuinely respectful

__ Spiritually open and aware

__ Physically healthy

__ Personal boundaries are clear

__ Often able to forgive self

__ Consciously present to others

__ Balances long—and short-term focus

__ Honest and open

__ Sensitive and empathic

__ Self-nurturing without being egotistical

__ Genuine in relationships

__ Receives praise easily

__ Can grieve losses and others

__ Able to share love honestly

__ Expresses feelings in the moment without major anxiety or guilt

---

❧**Notice:** Which traits did you check? Do they have something in common? For example, are most of the ones you checked related to attitude, to relationships, or to emotions? What do you notice? In what ways is your consciousness about yourself deepening?

_____

_____

_____

_____

Truth-Telling

When we deny or repress the truth about our feelings and memories, there is a kind of breaking apart, or *dis*integration, that takes place in our inner world, our psyche and moves us away from our wholeness. When we own our emotional truth, we promote healing and *re*integration of our psyche.

Owning our true feelings leads us to begin healing the pain. There are several ways in which we may do this: by changing our attitude or beliefs about something or someone, doing deeper work in ourselves with professional support, forgiving our self or someone else, or letting go of habits and practices that numb our pain. Healing and integration are about telling the truth.

Inner Work: The Way to Integration and Healing

Your integration process evolves because you are doing inner work. (You are doing some inner work in your Midlife Check-In process!) When your courage moves you to peer into yourself for a more intimate look at unexpressed parts, unmet emotional needs, discarded creative impulses, inner conflicts, limiting beliefs and fears, and unexplored gifts and talents, you are choosing to do inner work. You are also choosing to heal and become anchored in a place that is yours, and not somebody else's.

MY PERSONAL INTEGRATION: WHERE AM I?

To get a current sense of your inner self-awareness, integration, and healing processes take a look at the 16 pairs of statements that follow. Place an X on the scale between each pair to indicate what is most typical of your experience at this time in your life. It works best if you "go with your gut" to place your X. That feeling place has a "knowing" about you. Honest answers can be healing.

MY PERSONAL INTEGRATION: × ✐ WHERE AM I? ©
MarthaElin Mountain, Ed.D, M.A., MFT

Place an X on the scale between each of the 16 pairs to show where you feel you are currently.

The list of items on the right represents feelings and behaviors that come from a place of strong, conscious integration. The list of items on the left represents typical feelings and behaviors that come from a place of little or no conscious integration. Follow the directions for your next steps when you finish your self-assessment.

	1	2	3	4	5	
1. Inside I feel bored, empty, lonely, or unreal: fuzzy, confused	1	2	3	4	5	_I feel connected to the very "roots" of my being._
2. I appear successful and happy: inside I do not feel alive or real.	1	2	3	4	5	_I feel alive, creative, playful. Others have this sense of me._
3. I am afraid to feel my feelings. I live mostly in my head.	1	2	3	4	5	_I enjoy feeling my feelings, even if I do not express them._
4. I work to please others and to be what they want me to be	1	2	3	4	5	I express who I am, my true feelings and ideas.
5. I hide my True Self to protect me from possible criticism disapproval, or shame.	1	2	3	4	5	I am genuine in my relationships with others.
6. I mostly imitate other people's behavior to create a different image.	1	2	3	4	5	I can give myself to others without giving myself away.
7. I can take care of others but won't let myself feel dependent on others in any way.	1	2	3	4	5	I am comfortable accepting others' supportive gestures.
8. I am constantly "doing" because it feels safer than just "being."	1	2	3	4	5	I feel connected to my center or inner source. I can simply "be."

136

9. I feel very insecure when I don't have an answer.   1   2   3   4   5   I allow myself to be unsure, vulnerable, to "not know."

10. I expect something in return when I give to someone.   1   2   3   4   5   I give to others by choice, not because I am "supposed to."

11. My goal is to have things be "perfect."   1   2   3   4   5   I am comfortable with my best efforts.

12. I choose social relationships based mainly on status and image.   1   2   3   4   5   I choose genuine and reciprocal social relationships.

13. I make decisions for myself based on what I think others want.   1   2   3   4   5   I make decisions for myself unswayed by others' expectations.

14. I comply with others' wishes or demands because I feel I should.   1   2   3   4   5   I pay attention to my instincts for what feels "right" or not and make my choices accordingly.

15. I feel I must hide my honest feelings and pretend to be whatever others need me to be.   1   2   3   4   5   I am able to be my true Self within my relationships.

16. I do not like to play. I am too old to play. Playing is a waste of time.   1   2   3   4   5   Playing is an important and regular part of my life (making art, hobbies, sports, lively debate with friends).

DIRECTIONS: Beginning at the top of the 16 scales, scan downward to the end, noticing the pattern your X's made. What kind of pattern do you see: Pattern A, B, C, or D?

PATTERN A: <u>A fairly consistent pattern toward the left side?</u>

1	**X**	2	3	4	5
1	**X**	2	3	4	5
1	**X**	2	3	4	5

PATTERN B: <u>A fairly consistent pattern toward the right side?</u>

1	2	3		4	**X**	5
1	2	3	**X**	4		5
1	2	3		4	**X**	5

PATTERN C: <u>A fairly consistent pattern down the middle?</u>

1	2		3	**X**	4	5
1	2	**X**	3		4	5
1	2	**X**	3		4	5

PATTERN D: <u>A random pattern with no consistency?</u>

1	**X**	2		3		4	5
1		2		3	**X**	4	5
1		2	**X**	3		4	5

DIRECTIONS:

On the list below, find and ☑check the pattern your Xs made. Read the questions next to that pattern. Consider them thoughtfully. As you do, notice any sensations or cues your body seems to be giving you in response. Is there an inner "stirring up" of some kind? Is your body remembering a particular experience? Do you feel moved in some other way? What self-talk are you hearing? Take note of these . . . .

☐ **PATTERN A:** Of the 16 feelings and behaviors listed on the right side, which of them seem to be the most uncomfortable for you? Acknowledge these as personal challenges for you at this time. Identify examples of 1 or 2 people in real life, film, novels, or art who you believe would place their X's closer to the right side. Consider what traits they have that you would like to develop in yourself. Remember to acknowledge the admirable traits you possess and the times and ways you have been true to yourself.

---

*✍ **NOTE** You may want to seek professional support to: a) clarify what seems to keep your Xs closer to the left side, b) heal any fears and or emotional issues that keep your Xs closer to the left side, c) learn ways to become increasingly comfortable with who you really are.*

☐ **PATTERN B:** Of all the answers you marked, which behavior or feeling seems to be easiest for you? Which ones have you been working on most in your life? Which ones are the most challenging for you at home? At work? With friends? Notice what you are feeling especially good about in your pattern of answers. What stands out most for you?

☐ **PATTERN C:** Of all the answers you marked, which ones would you like most to change and to improve? Which ones are you most aware of in your family life? Work life? Social life? Which of the feelings and behaviors do you believe have improved over time? Are there any that you want to work on or change in some way either now or in the future?

☐ **PATTERN D:** Which of the feelings and behaviors make the most difference in your life at home, at work, in your relationships? Which ones seem to be working *for* you? *Against* you? If you were going to choose one feeling or behavior to shift in yourself, which one would it be? What kind of shift do you want to see? How can you begin to make this happen?

Now that you have read and considered the questions next to the pattern of your Xs, what did you observe? What feelings are moving around in you? What might your next steps be? Turn to the Back Pocket or your personal notebook and make a note of these things.

---

3. THE NOT-KNOWING:
Being in the Place Without Answers

- Visualization
- Wondering

"You must be able to hang . . . between sky and earth if you want to solve problems."
Carl G. Jung

Your search for answers to the question who am I *really?* will always include the "not-knowing," the place in you without answers. It is the place in you and me that knows more than we do and that is more than we are.

Being in the space of not-knowing can leave you feeling anchorless, unmoored. Without concrete answers, you are likely to feel baffled, insecure, or embarrassed. You want to understand something and cannot pin it down. Your curiosity is raised, but with no clear sense of direction. Expect this. It comes with the process of deepening inner awareness.

The following Practice with Visualization is designed to help you connect with your place of not-knowing. So, pause here. Take a deep breath. Let it out very s-l-o-w-l-y. Then, begin the exercise.

Visualization

When we create a picture or get a sense of something in our mind, we give it life. We also make it our own. It is an image or feeling with personal meaning, of how we "see" something from our experience or inner perspective. Try this out to see what happens when you close your eyes and "visualize" an apple? Are you primarily seeing it? sensing it? or feeling what it is like? Any and all of these can happen when we "visualize" something.

The following exercise, "Practice with Visualization," will help you make the idea of Not-Knowing a more tangible.

Practice with Visualization

"The image itself by the sheer force of its presence can change us to the core."
Marion Woodman

1. Take a moment to pause and just sit quietly. Focus on the place of Not-Knowing in you, where you feel adrift. Notice what moves through your mind and what sensations you feel in your body when you consider the Not-Knowing. Really notice. Get a feel for your experience, without words.

2. Now imagine: What does Not-Knowing, the place in you without answers, seem to look like? What shape or form do you feel it has? What colors do you see when you imagine "not-knowing" energy?

3. Notice if it seems to be: hollow? dense? airy? or contained in some way?

4. If you could touch Not-Knowing, what texture might it have: smooth and velvety? rough? lacey? scratchy?

5. What kind of energy do you feel when you think of that Not-Knowing place in you: calm? intense? soothing? nonjudgmental?

6. In your mind or in the space below, create an image of Not-Knowing based on what you imagined and felt:

When you find yourself in the space of Not-Knowing, your likely response may be to try to come up with an answer, to find something to fill the void. When you can't, you may want to get out of the space. You may feel like giving up.

Your best response to being in Not-Knowing, however, is not to give up. It is just to *"be"* in it, to bob up and down in it, to trust it and let it move *you*. When you allow yourself to be moved around in this space, with no familiar answers, you soften and relax, and the experience becomes workable. How can you do that? How can you stay *with* your not-knowing and let it instruct you? You can do it by wondering, by letting your curiosity lead you.

Wondering

Wondering opens the door to possibilities for making sense of what eludes your rational mind. When you wonder, you invite useful hints or clues to come through to you. And they do "come through"—via your imagination, insights, gut feelings, dreams, "chance" encounters, images, colors, and symbols!

Practice with Wondering

Wonder: What if the Not-Knowing place could speak to you with words? What might it say? What do you think it would want you to know? Hmmm . . .

Wonder: What insights might be possible for you to gather in the place of Not-Knowing that are not available to you in other places of your life?

Wonder: What might come forward, do you think, if you simply relaxed and bobbed up and down in the Not-Knowing without any pressure on yourself?

Wonder: What might change for you if you embraced Not-Knowing?

If, *instead* of wondering, you respond to not-knowing by pushing hard for answers *now*, you actually push away the clues and other helpful information that may be suspended just outside of your awareness. When you push against this space, instead of bobbing up and down in it and wondering, you derail your search for Self.

Focusing on the Positives

• Golden Nuggets: Unseen Assets
• Some of My Unseen Nuggets
• Shadow Nuggets

GOLDEN NUGGETS: Unseen Assets

As it is with wholeness, the golden nuggets within you are a blend of things seen and unseen. This Golden Nuggets exercise aims to focus your attention on nuggets you may not have thought about, witnessed, or *felt*. These might include: hidden potential, personal vitality, images of role models, unexpressed creativity, and/or emotional clarity about something.

Pausing to sit under your Tree of Midlife and reflect can help you be in touch with many of the golden nuggets you have. You identified some nuggets in the two preceding chapters. Some of these are gifts from your years before midlife. Others are resources gleaned from more recent experiences. Your golden nuggets have emerged from triumphs, specific skills, relationship challenges, talents, and insights from mistakes made.

Some of My Unseen Nuggets

The following questions are prompts for the kind of self-reflection you might do while leaning against your Tree of Midlife. So, climb down and lean against the tree. Relax. Open yourself to what may show up in response to each question below.

Inner responses may come through images, memories, words, visions, body sensations, flashes of insight, and a kind of "knowing." Trust your gut and that wise part in you that wants to be "heard."

Directions

1. Take a long, slow, deep breath in and exhale gently.
2. Ask the question, directing it to a deeper part of you. If it helps you, close your eyes while you ask the question.
3. Breathe deeply and gently, and wait.
4. Allow space for whatever might come to you. Trust that a response (brief or longer) will come to you in its own time, if not now, later.
5. Write down or draw whatever you "get."

Question	Inner Response
1. What are my 2-3 greatest personal strengths?	
2. When does my true vitality express itself?	
3. What lies dormant in me that wants to develop?	
4. What is it like when I feel my own inner spark of enthusiasm?	
5. What is something of great value I have learned in life?	
6. How can I tell when it is my intuition that brings me insight?	

7. When do I experience
   insight and clarity most?

8. What part of me has been
   hidden for a long time
   and wants to emerge?

9. Where does my courage lie?

10. How can I tell when
    my authentic Self is in
    charge?

Shadow Nuggets

Some of the pure gold you were born with has been relegated to hidden corners in you, what we call the "shadow" aspects of your personality.

When we grow up in a culture that insists that we behave in a certain manner, we usually put away some of our natural behaviors and instincts because they seem unacceptable. We learn at an early age which parts of our authentic Self are acceptable. We sort out the characteristics or elements of our pure gold (authentic) nature into two groups: those that are acceptable to our culture and those that we must refuse or put away.

Question #8 in the preceding exercise addresses part of this. An important task for us in midlife and later years is to get our golden nuggets out of the shadow!

Can you think of aspects of yourself that you have "put away" and that you would like to bring to life? Jot them down:

_____

_____

_____

Exploring My Identity

• **Sorting Out Who I Am**
• **Roles and False Assumptions**
• **A Symbol of Who I Am *Really***

Sorting Out Who I Am

Sorting out who you really are is an ongoing process of sorting what is yours from what is not yours. It is an "inside" job that we begin early in life and it can shift our sense of self as we mature. From our midlife years onward there is an increasing sense of urgency in this task of sorting. We ask ourselves Why am I here? Who am I apart from my history and the roles I have played? What makes me who I am?

The exercise, "Traits Associated with Being Real," is a good example of a task that requires you to sort. You identified which of the listed traits are true for you at this time, leaving out the rest. In the exercise, "My Personal Integration: Where Am I?" you had to sort out if certain feelings and behaviors resonate for you, so that you could mark what is true for you on each of the 16 scales.

Sorting was also involved with several earlier exercises in this book. In some you had to decide what is or is not true about you. In others, you had to come up with specific attributes to describe yourself. For example, in the "My Identity" exercises of the two previous chapters, three of the factors you considered about yourself are important clues to who you are really: 1) "Roles," 2) "Hopes, dreams, and ideals that I aspire to," and 3) "The message I most want others to 'get'." You can revisit these in Chapters Eight and Nine.

When Are You Sorting?

Sorting happens in various circumstances. You are sorting when you are:

- Reflecting on something you did in the past, why you did it, and what you might do differently in the future
- Making a major decision or choice
- Wrestling with conflicting feelings about something
- Pondering something significant that you know you will have to say to someone
- Having your views or beliefs challenged by someone who has strong arguments against them

---

In these circumstances you are turning over inside of you the possibilities and choices to see which one or ones *feel right* to you. You are getting a sense of how you feel about something you might do or that you did. "Does this feel right to me?" "What can I live with?" "How will I feel about my decision later?" are questions we might ask when we are sorting. How you answer these questions is a reflection of who you are from the inside-out.

Sometimes something you felt "right" about at the time you did it turns out, in hindsight, not to feel so right to you. Feelings of regret or guilt can emerge and prompt you to reconsider: "What would I do differently in the future?" "What feels more truthful to me now?" "How can I accept what I did, let it go, and move forward?" When answered honestly, all of these questions are part of your sorting process, moving you closer to your identity from the inside-out.

• One of the most difficult sorting experiences I remember having is

_____

• A sorting experience that moved me to make major changes or take a different path from before is

_____

• A sorting experience I would change today if I could is

_____

What I would do differently in that situation is

_____

Sorting Shifts Your Identity

Over time, your sorting experiences lead to shifts in your sense of self and how you live your life. This is because wrestling honestly with decisions and choices and becoming aware of what is real in you help you to develop insight. Your increasing consciousness and your motivation to become more authentic shift you. With each shift you make, consciously or not, you grow closer to wholeness.

As you review your responses to exercises in previous parts of this book and you consider who you have been and who you are now, in what ways has your sense of self remained the same or changed?

Same sense of self: _____

_____

Changed sense of self: _____

_____

The more you work at sorting out who you are from who you are not, the more likely you are to develop a connection with who you are *really*. Bit by bit, sorting works to peel off the layers of a persona that has protected your authentic Self. As the layers come off, you deepen your connection with the person you were meant to be; you become more of who you are meant to become. We call this developmental process "individuation."

Kinds of Shifts You Make

There are various kinds of shifts you might make in the ongoing course of sorting what is yours from what is not (or, who you are from who you are not). Look at the examples below.

Have you made any of these shifts?

- Breaking away from a particular group, partnership, or set of values that no longer holds meaning or resonates for you
- Responding to a "calling" to pursue a particular interest or vocation
- Giving deeper expression to your creative impulses
- Being in touch with others in more genuine, or real, ways
- Feeling more in touch with your body, embracing its
- sensations and processes as part of who you are
- Being more spontaneous and playful
- Protecting personal time for quiet and reflection.

<u>My Own Shifts</u>

• Perhaps you recognize some of the shifts listed above or others that you have made? ✐ Jot down personal shifts you are aware of:

_____

_____

_____

• What shifts may you be making at this time in your life?

_____

_____

_____

• What is it like for you in a time of shift? What feelings are you aware of inside?

_____

_____

_____

• When you are making a shift what changes seem to happen *around* you and in your life?

_____

_____

_____

• How have your shifts helped you to connect to something more "real" in you? What changes have you noticed in yourself?

_____

_____

_____

ROLES AND FALSE ASSUMPTIONS

<u>Roles</u>

Over the course of our lives, we have probably used a variety of external markers to stake out our identity: our name or family, relationships, achievements, personality, and who others say we are. Sometimes, we have let our emotional needs (e.g. to be loved) and our unhealthy strategies (e.g. take on role of victim or helpless one) define us.

We have played different roles. Sometimes we have *become* a role (e.g. perfectionist, parent, lover, comedienne, peacemaker, child, helper, employee, dependent one, etc.), and we have let it create our identity. We have confused the face we show in the world with the Self we are really. This is understandable, considering that the choices we made in our first 20-30 years were made when we were learning to fit in, to find a place for ourselves in the world, to create an identity.

<u>Here is an example of an experience in which a woman could easily have confused her ego's sense of identity with who she is really:</u>

A friend in her early seventies, was invited to participate in a community fashion show. Glamorous outfits were selected for her to model. In preparation for the event, she was "made up" with cosmetics intended to give her a more glamorous and stunning appearance.

She described her inner experience to me later: "I was all dolled up. Shortly before going out on the runway, I glanced in the mirror at myself. I was taken aback! 'Who is this?' I thought. I realized, at once, that this person looking back at me is the person I *could* have been, if I had chosen earlier in my life to be a status-conscious woman.

If I had, this is the kind of role I would have played, the personality I would have lived. I would have focused on my physical appearance as a way to impress others. I would have confused my appearance with who I am. In that instant of looking in the mirror, I realized how *unlike* that reflected image I truly am."

False Assumptions

Confusing who we are with a role or other external marker leads us to make false assumptions about out identity. Below are some examples of false assumptions we may make. Notice if any of them seem familiar.

ARE ANY OF THESE FALSE ASSUMPTIONS MINE?

- My body and physical appearance represent who I am.
- My age and circumstances create my identity.
- The role I play is who I am.
- The career I choose is who I am.
- Being compliant is who I am.
- My emotional or behavioral challenges label who I am.
- How others see me defines who I am.

NOTICE: Which assumptions caught your attention? Consider any that may have defined your identity at some time in your life. Are there any that you use sometimes to define you now?

_____

_____

_____

❖

A SYMBOL OF WHO I AM—*REALLY*

As mentioned previously, there are times when we may have a feeling about something but do not have words to express it adequately. An experience may touch or move us deeply, or some deeper place in us "knows" what we mean but does not have words to express it. In this exercise you will identify a symbol of who you sense yourself to be—*really*.

While working with the focus question in this chapter, feelings, beliefs, energy, and/or values about who you are *really* may have emerged. Recall the earlier discussion in this chapter about "integration." Do you remember the space of overlap that develops in you, at a deeper level, as your self-awareness of ego and some of the veiled aspects of yourself increases?

As an inner shift of this sort takes place, it is hard for us to find words to help us make sense of it. A meaning or understanding of something has changed for us. We feel the shift and its inner impact, but we do not have words to explain what it means. We feel afloat, unanchored, in the experience. Finding a symbol for your experience can be very helpful. It is a tangible connection with it.

Consider "who" you are—really. What inner sense do you have of her? What symbol that you know (or might create) could represent the deeper meaning or sense *you* have of who you are—*really*?

If nothing comes to mind, look around your environments for objects and ideas. Browse magazines and online image collections. Look at designs on book covers. Look at images in nature. What jumps out at you? What may hold some or all of the meaning of who you are really?

Choose something. Make a note or put the image in the Back Pocket or in your personal notebook. In the last part of the book, Part Four, you will bring together this symbol and the two you identified in earlier.

Digging Deeper

- **Ten Below**
- **Notice and Reflect**
- **Holes and Empty Places:**
Your Unseen Shadow Self

TEN BELOW

The 10 statements below can help you dig deeper. They can connect you with aspects of your life and who you are *really* that you may or may not have thought about recently.

As you read each statement, be spontaneous; fill in what comes to mind first. If you cannot think of something to write, go on to the remaining items and come back. The best approach is to work from your gut. The best policy is total honesty. Remember: this is for YOU!

☐ **1.** I notice that I feel most "at home" and at peace with myself when I

_____

_____

☐ **2.** I feel a deep love for myself when

_____

_____

☐ **3.** I express myself from a deeper place within me, and without concern for what others may think, when

_____

_____

☐ **4.** When I cannot find words to express how I feel about someone or something I care about, I notice that I

_____

_____

☐ **5.** I can tell that I have a "gut feeling" about something when I

_____

_____

☐ **6.** Something that is difficult for me and is hard to find words for is

_____

_____

☐ **7.** An image or a symbol that "speaks" to me or moves me deeply is

_____

_____

☐ **8.** I can sense that something "deep" is going on inside of me when

_____

_____

☐ **9.** I can sense the times when I am seeking more meaning for my life because I

_____

_____

☐ **10.** If I were told today that I had one year left to live,

_____

_____ would matter deeply to me.

✎ NOTICE and REFLECT

Review the 10 statements you completed above:

Notice:

• Which statements were easy for you to answer?
• Which statements were especially difficult for you to answer?
☑ Put a check next to them.

✍ NOTE: *A strong, uncomfortable reaction to completing a statement may suggest that something in you cries out for mending; there may be "unfinished business" that needs resolution. If so, seeking professional support may be appropriate for you.*

Reflect:

• Do any concerns or issues call out to you to be resolved? If you keep a journal, work with the arts, have a meditation practice or other quiet time, consider using one of the statements you checked as a focus for reflection.

✏ <u>Jot down what you notice about your responses:</u>

_____

_____.

_____

HOLES AND EMPTY PLACES:
Your Unseen Shadow Self

✍ *NOTE: If you are currently dealing with a personal crisis or another emotional upheaval, please consider working on the following exercise in partnership with a licensed therapist. Or, come back to this when you feel grounded.*

"Find out what a person fears most and that is where (s)he will develop next."
C.G. Jung
<u>Our basic emotional needs include:</u>

- <u>feeling loved</u>
- <u>feeling we belong</u>
- <u>feeling safe</u>
- <u>feeling worthy</u>

During your midlife years, and certainly at other times in life, you may find yourself in a period of increased upheaval and "testing." This is sometimes called "the dark night of the soul." It is during this period that you might feel as if certain aspects of yourself, ones that you have "managed" and kept out of sight for many years, are running amuck. What is stirring inside of you may be feeling completely unfamiliar. When you start to experience yourself in this whole new way, you can bet that it is your shadow who has come to visit!

This typically happens more in midlife because that is when your deeper needs and values are changing direction. Unexpressed parts of your true nature are seeking ways to express themselves. You are being called to break old habits, loosen the reins, and give attention to the neglected parts of yourself. You are being called to confront and acknowledge your shadow.

You were growing your shadow during the years before midlife. From now on, however, you must come to know and integrate these discarded or neglected parts of you, if you are to grow into wholeness. It is a challenge and you cannot approach it with *thinking* alone. To understand this new experience in yourself, you must confront it and get to know it through inner work. When you learn how to meet and manage your shadow in healthy ways, what you discover are hidden allies.

Benefits of Meeting Your Shadow's Challenge

Confronting and understanding your shadow elements has many benefits. The primary one is your ever-widening consciousness about who you really are. Other important benefits include:

- A growing realization of your inner strength and confidence
- A sense of compassion for yourself and others
- Increasing openness to engaging your creative energies
- Stronger decision and action behaviors
- Softening of the edges around your ego, which makes it stronger and better able to manage your emotions.

Our Defenses Against Shadow

As individuals we rely on various ways to keep the shadow under control, instead of bearing it and assimilating it as part of our true Self. For example, we work long hours, take antidepressant drugs to dampen our despair, find numerous ways to be distracted by other people, and create a persona.

Our society relies on a variety of ways to help us contain the shadow. For example, we make horror movies, create violent images, market risqué clothing, publish racy novels, and write shocking headlines. These are ways people can see or experience shadow elements without acknowledging them as parts of themselves.

Individually we rely on projection to contain our shadow. We cast simple projections, or judgments, on our partners or friends, without realizing it is usually something in us waiting to be expressed. We point out flaws and short-comings in others. Or, we have those days when we are reactive to store clerks, the bank teller, our children, or our boss. We are unaware that it is not really them—it is us having a difficult day. Our shadow is expressing itself.

Contrary to what you might expect, your shadow is not "evil." It is actually closer to the center of your true Self and more genuine than your ego. Any fear or resistance you may feel about your shadow elements is actually your ego's doing. It wants to keep you in its "ideal" world, as it did during your pre-midlife years. Now, perhaps, things are going to change.

When we leave our shadow aspects in our unconscious and do nothing conscious about them, they turn up in our emotions and behaviors in any number of ways: rudeness, depression, prejudice, loneliness, rage, shame, an intense reaction to a quality in someone, boredom, an ill temper, inner emptiness, slips of the tongue or behavior, psychosomatic illness, substance abuse, and a various defensive behaviors, just to name a few.

All the shadow wants is to be acknowledged so it can transform into your ally.

Defenses

We are not always aware of our defensive strategies that are holding us back. We brought them with us from childhood to adulthood. We developed them to defend ourselves and to cope with the world as we knew it. Now, in our adult lives these behaviors limit us.

The list below names a variety of self-defeating behaviors. ☑ Put a check by any of the defensive behaviors below that you recognize from your past or present life:

<u>Defensive Behaviors</u>

___ Appearing to be very busy, but accomplishing little

___ Gossiping

___ Giving up, retreating from competition

___ Being incompetent to avoid meeting expectations

___ Relying on substances to feel good

___ Holding back positive behaviors and qualities

___ Depending on a role, an image, or others' approval

___ Withholding effort

___ Being "forgetful"

___ Playing the victim, expressed in childish ways

___ Using achievements to compensate for low self-esteem

___ Self-sabotage via procrastination, disorganization, or
    non-productive working style

___ Acting in ways that reflect how my parent(s) defined me

<u>Facing What Is Difficult for You</u>

In life, you are given repeated opportunities to confront and acknowledge your shadow: to face what you fear, what you need to master, or what you need to become conscious of about yourself. When a particularly challenging person or situation "gets" to you, you might look for ways to avoid her, or to get away from it. You might even consider leaving your place of work or changing relationships to do so. Or, you might distract yourself with food or substances. In the end, however, no matter how clever you think you are in avoiding it, the same or a similar negative challenge will show up, once again, and greet you.

<u>Repeated Encounters</u>

Thus, in life you return to what is difficult for you until you learn healthy ways to deal with it. Ideally, each time you return to a difficulty (or it returns to you), your consciousness increases and you are able to respond to it with more clarity and wisdom. What is difficult for you to handle will continue to present itself until you develop enough awareness and learn how to manage it with inner confidence and peace.

My Own Repeated Encounter:
Three Questions

Question 1: What personal challenge have you met up with more than once in your life that is hard for you and that you tend to shy away from? What situation or type of person draws a negative response from you and keeps returning in various ways to challenge you?

_____

_____

_____

Question 2: What might you be learning about yourself from this challenge? What do you think it is trying to teach or show you?

_____

_____

_____

Question 3: How might your experience with this challenge help you become a guide for others?

_____

_____

_____

Your Shadow Transforms

Something very curious about your shadow is that when you have the courage to look at a disowned part—it changes! As you bring it up into your conscious awareness, your neglected part becomes softer and gentler; it is more pliable. This process is taking place in your ego, or personality, at the same time. Being acknowledged and "seen" is what your shadow has been waiting for. By honoring your shadow elements and allowing them to speak to you they no longer need to get your attention in ways that are uncomfortable or that feel negative to you and others. A transformation has taken place.

Transforming with Wisdom

When you arrive at your midlife years you have a kind of wisdom developing in you that helps you to be conscious about your shortcomings and the unfinished business you may have in you.

You may come to a place where you have had enough of being stuck and dealing repeatedly with the same annoying challenges or self-defeating behaviors. You may desire a more peaceful or authentic way of being. Being at this turning point can open you to healing and growth. Just *opening* to the possibility of inner change allows your ego and your unseen Self to begin to teach each other something. A "call" comes forth from inside of you to grow.

Gathering the courage to explore your shadow elements is a primary task of your midlife years and beyond. These elements are, after all, your potential allies. Once transformed, they will help you in your process of becoming more of the person you are meant to be.

Being Open to Blending

When you open yourself to healing and growth and do the inner work, you encourage your integration process. Hidden between your shadow life and the ideal life your ego works so hard to live is a place of integration, a place where they can come together, over time. (It is the same place I described, earlier in this chapter, as a container or womb for new growth in you.) As your consciousness grows, your insight grows, and emotional healing begins to take place.

Place of Integration

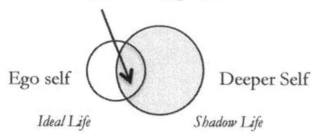

Ego self · Deeper Self

Ideal Life · *Shadow Life*

On the other hand, if you resist the painful or uncomfortable places inside of you by numbing yourself with work, substances, busyness, or other distractions, you close off the possibilities for healing. You remain stuck in your ego or small self and you do not grow; your ego and deeper Self remain in opposition with one another. As a result, they create emotional and behavioral conflicts, both inside of you and out in the world.

Bridge-Building

As you open to the inner work for your healing and growth, a connection between the competing ego self and deeper Self starts to form. A kind of bridge or walkway is under construction between them. As you continue your inner work and move toward emotional healing and new growth, both you and the bridge become stronger. It becomes possible for you to bear more of the weight of life's challenges and to manage it in healthy, balanced ways.

Centered and Balanced

Do you remember my earlier reference to a woman who seems "centered and balanced?" the woman who comes across as genuine, who feels safe with who she is? This is the woman who functions much of the time from her inner place of integration. She is present. In the exercise "Traits Associated with Being Real" you identified the traits you recognize in yourself, even if only on occasion. When these traits come alive in you, you are standing in the middle of the bridge between your ideal, or ego self, and your shadow. Where you stand, in the middle and in balance, is the place of your authentic or true Self. It is the balancing point for your integration process.

Standing on Your Bridge

This bridge between your small self (small "s") and your deeper, wiser Self (Big "S") is a continuum of possibilities between the ideas and energies that oppose one another in you. Ideally, it is a place to stand and center yourself. While the idea of doing this sounds simple, it is not so easy to achieve. The tension between opposites is always there for you to reckon with. You are continuously pulled in life toward one end of the bridge or the other. The world beckons you in this direction and that. As you develop your capacity to stand in the middle of the bridge, you are increasingly able to hold this tension between your ego and your deeper Self. As you do, you let go of the need to judge.

Standing in this place on the bridge means holding opposites simultaneously. Right and wrong, knowing and not-knowing, light and dark, masculine and feminine, creative and destructive, are a few examples of opposites. Being in the center of the bridge involves balancing and integrating—like holding both water and dirt and integrating them with our hands to make mud. We can do things with mud that neither water nor dirt can do alone. It is what we call "both, and." Each element brings its unique qualities to the other and blending makes them something more. Something new is created, holding more possibilities. Thus, "both, *and.*"

Holding the Opposites:
An Example with Masculine and Feminine

I will use the opposites of feminine and masculine to provide an example of "holding the opposites." Both of these natures reside in every human being; we each have masculine and feminine elements. Over the years, we may have developed one of them much more than the other, allowing one to dominate our approach to living. Nature's intention, however, is a healthy balance between them.

Certain behaviors and ways of thinking and feeling are associated with feminine or masculine energy. Some of these associations include:

Feminine Nature	**Masculine Nature**
Creativity	Determination
Nurturing	Courage
Intuition	Concrete Thinking
Compassion	Either-or Thinking
Empathy	Assertion
Openness to Possibility	Aggression
Sensitivity	Domination
Patience	Urgency

When you stand on the midpoint of your bridge, you can draw on your feminine and masculine natures in ways that are positive, constructive, and balanced. For example, at a meeting of colleagues where the opinion you hold about something differs from others', you can acknowledge the value and interesting aspects in others' views *(openness, empathy)* without putting them down *(aggression)*. You can state your own view with passion and clarity *(assertion)*.

Your decision to engage in the Midlife Check-In process is another example of drawing in positive ways from your masculine and feminine natures. You asserted *(masculine)* your desire to deepen your sense of Self by choosing this book, while being open *(feminine)* to the unknown and possibilities in the Check-In process.

When you work to integrate such opposites in you, no matter what you are doing, you experience your most authentic energy—what some would call your divine energy. Doing this frees and renews you. You thrive; your soul thrives. And there is heart in what you do.

Moving toward your place of integration and authentic nature is a deepening in understanding and acceptance of who you really are. This deepening leads you inward to a more balanced and peaceful place from which to live your midlife years and beyond.

Checking in:
My Comfort Level and Feelings

• Where Am I?
• Feelings Gauge
• 21 Ways to Take Care of Myself Right Now

✗ ✐ WHERE AM I?

Place an X on the (1-5) scale below to show your comfort level:

I am extremely __uncomfortable__ exploring who I am really.

I am extremely __comfortable__ exploring who I am really.

1_____2_____3_____4_____5

I put my X very close to :

☐ **5 or 4:** Continue to explore your inner world experiences and deeper beliefs that reflect who you really are. With trusted guidance and support (preferably professional), identify your shadow elements that are calling for attention and transformation.

☐ **3:** Pay attention to the communications from your unconscious that you are most comfortable with. Identify positive and safe ways to work with them. For example: Read about the unconscious, dreams, instincts, and the shadow. Notice experiences and feelings that are uncomfortable for you. Use writing, the arts, and professional support to help you understand and work with them.

☐ **2 or 1:** (You may want to) seek professional support to **a)** sort out and clarify what you are defending against **b)** define and address fears and conflicts, and/or **c)** heal "stuffed" emotional pain.

Look over the recommendations next to your choice of comfort level (**5 or 4**; **3**; **2 or 1**). Circle a recommendation you would like to follow through on. Make a note of it in your notebook or in the Back Pocket for future reference. When will you follow through?

What Are You Feeling—*In This Moment?*

Pause, now. Notice the sensations or "messages" your body is giving to you *in this moment*. Do a quick body scan: Begin at the top of your head. Notice your scalp, eyes, and jaw area. Is there tightness anywhere? Notice your shoulders: Are they pulled forward, or are they relaxed and down? Scan your torso, each arm and hand, and both legs and feet. Is there tension anywhere?

If you notice any tension or discomfort, such as tightness, pain, or churning, where is it in your body? Be sure to notice, also, which part of your body is most relaxed. Just notice . . . and breathe.

Use the Feelings Gauge below to help you zero in on your feelings *in this moment*.

FEELINGS GAUGE:
WHAT AM I FEELING, *RIGHT NOW?*

Circle the number on the scale below that best describes how you are feeling *right now, in this very moment.* **0** represents the calmest feeling state and **10** represents the most upset feeling state. Descriptions of associated body sensations are shown at each extreme to help you gauge where your feelings are *in this moment.*

0 . . .**1** . . .**2** . . .**3** . . .**4** . . .**5** . . .**6** . . .**7** . . .**8** . . .**9** . . .**10**

Clear	Confused
Centered	Scattered
Relaxed, Still	Tense, Agitated
Nonjudgmental	Reactive, Critical
Slow deep breathing	Rapid breathing
Resting pulse rate	Fast pulse
In total peace	On high alert

✍ **NOTE:** If you experience feelings of distress while engaged in a Midlife Check-In exercise, these feelings may be a signal to you that it is time to take a break and relax. Symptoms of distress may include one or more of the following: sweaty palms, tension building in your chest, throat tightening, jaw clenching, breathing on hold, nausea, tears, urge to scream or yell, head aching.

Use the following list, "21 Ways to Take Care of Myself Right Now," for suggestions of specific ways to calm yourself in the moment. If painful feelings like these are hard for you to manage in healthy ways, consider seeking professional support.

21 WAYS I CAN TAKE CARE OF MYSELF
RIGHT NOW ©

It is important to have simple and effective ways to manage your tension and uncomfortable feelings in the moment. Below are 21 ideas for doing so. Using these can help you move quickly toward a more relaxed and balanced state of being.

☑ Check the ones you like most:

☐ Breathe deeply and slowly

☐ Move freely to music

☐ Stand, stretch, walk around

☐ Do 10-20 jumping jacks

☐ Bend gently side to side, then forward slightly

☐ Beat a drum

☐ Light a candle and be with its light for a few minutes

☐ Hold or stroke my pet

☐ Move to a different space

☐ Watch a funny movie about myself

☐ Climb into my midlife tree

☐ Be in nature near flowers, trees, water, soothing views

☐ Hug myself and breathe

☐ Ring my singing bowl

☐ Speak with a trusted friend

☐ Drink a warm beverage such as herbal tea, milk, soup

☐ Laugh out loud

☐ Shift my body position and breathe deeply

☐ Place my hands over my heart

☐ Focus on an inspiring image

☐ Make a positive statement

Midlife Glossary:
Check Out These Words

Below is a list of glossary words you may wish to explore in relation to this chapter. ☑ Put a check by any that "call" to you, and find their meanings in the Midlife Glossary. How might the words relate to *who you are* really?

☐ anima	☐ not-knowing
☐ animus	☐ psyche
☐ consciousness	☐ Self
☐ defenses	☐ shadow
☐ dream	☐ unconscious
☐ gnosis	☐ visualization
☐ integration	☐ wholeness
☐ intuition	☐ wonder

Leaning Against My Midlife Tree

"Only in solitude can you discover your own beauty."
John O'Donohue

• Sit and Reflect
• Back Pocket

What captured my attention most?
What puzzled or concerned me?
What do I want to explore further?
How can who I am really affect my life today?

Sit and Reflect

Take a few moments now to climb down from your personal tree of midlife to lean against it or sit under it and reflect on the question, "Who am I *really*?" When you are in a comfortable spot, take a relaxation belly breath, and let it out s-l-o-w-l-y.

Open to a few quiet moments with yourself, with no expectations. Consider the work you have done in this chapter "Who Am I *Really*?" and ask yourself the four questions listed above. Consider the colors and patterns the Seven Threads of Becoming might be weaving at a deeper level inside of you.

In this space of conversation with yourself insights may grab your attention, questions may surface, or ideas for personal actions may materialize. Who knows? Just relax for a few minutes in your own company while being in the protective shade of your midlife tree. Be . . . and breathe.

Back Pocket

Turn to the Back Pocket or your personal notebook and jot down any thoughts, questions, or insights that may have moved through you. How might the symbols you chose earlier reflect them?

You may wish to use one or more of the following ways to give "voice" to your reflections about who you are *really*. What calls to you: music, drawing, collage, painting, expressive movement, poetry or other writing?

Congratulations!

You have completed Part Three, the heart of your Midlife Check-In process. My hope is that working with the exercises in Part Three has expanded your Self awareness and deepened your consciousness about who you have been, who you are now, and who you are *really*.

Everything you have noticed, learned, and reflected upon in your Check-In process helps to ground you in a deeper, truer sense of yourself. It opens you to new possibilities for who and how you want to become in the next years and decades of your life.

Part Four invites you to stand at the helm of your midlife journey and ask "Who and how do I imagine myself becoming?"

FOUR

Now What? Who and How Am I Becoming?

Introduction

Chapter Eleven
Five Brief Exercises

Chapter Twelve
I Imagine Myself Becoming Someone Who . . .

"Get out of your comfort zone. Try new things—classes, groups, painting—who knows what will inspire you!."

Barbara, Full-Moon Woman, age 78

Introduction

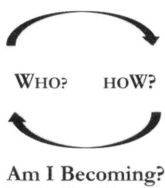

WHO? HOW?

Am I Becoming?
(Based on Who I Have Been,
Who I Am Now, and Who I Am *Really*)

> *"I am not what happened to me; I am what I choose to become."*
> James Hollis

In Part Three, you climbed down from your tree of midlife to reflect consciously on questions about who you have been, who you are now, and who you are *really*. While sitting under your tree or leaning against it in reflection, you shifted your vantage point and opened yourself to the possibility of new observations, insights, and questions.

You also opened yourself to the process of integration. Becoming open in this way allowed a kind of exchange to take place between your outside experiences and your inner, perhaps deeper, ones. While you were in this space of conversation with yourself, new questions may have bubbled up, insights may have appeared, or ideas for taking action may have stepped forward.

Now, it is time to climb back up into your tree for a bird's-eye view of the information, ideas, insights, and questions you have gathered and tucked into your Back Pocket, personal notebook, or the back of your mind. This information is extremely valuable; it will help you clarify qualities of your authentic Self—who you are meant to become.

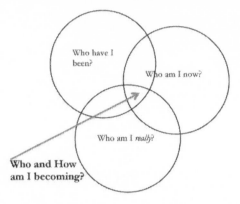

Next Steps in Becoming

Who is the more authentic Self you imagine becoming? If I asked you to name the qualities of this person, what words might you choose? What image of her or him might you imagine? How would she or he move? Use his or her voice?

Allow a sense of your more authentic Self to evolve . . . Feel this person stirring in you . . . and listen for the voice that no one—not even you—has heard before.

In Chapter Eleven, you will enlarge and deepen your understanding of the more authentic person you imagine becoming. You will:

- Go into your heart and play
- Look into your Back Pocket
- Explore obstacles and stumbling blocks
- Consider what needs repairing or mending
- Gather your resources

You will also check in with your feelings, using the "Feelings Gauge" exercise.

You may wish to extend your knowledge and deepen your understanding of midlife by exploring "Midlife Glossary: Check Out These Words." Find their meanings in the Midlife Glossary.

⏀ NOTE: If, at any time, while engaging in this chapter, you do not feel comfortable with what comes up, turn to "21 Ways to Take Care of Myself Right Now" on page 199 and follow the directions. Take a break. Check in with a professional, if your discomfort continues and interferes with your daily functioning.

Chapter Eleven

FIVE BRIEF EXERCISES

- **Look into Your Heart and Play**
- **Look into Your Back Pocket**
- **Obstacles and Stumbling Blocks**
- **Repairs and Mendings**
- **My Resources for Becoming**

"Let nothing dim the light that shines from within."
Maya Angelou

The BIG question you will always be working with in your process of becoming more true to your Self, and the question to ask yourself now is:

Who is the natural, authentic Self I am meant to become more of—*the one who longs to be expressive in creative and heartful ways? The one with important dreams to fulfill and truths to share?*

Your more authentic identity is not about an idealized personal image. It is about the natural self that you possessed as a child. Being authentic means following the wisdom of the instincts you were born with. It means joining with the inner part of you that is free from self-judgments and the judgments of others.

Your more authentic identity is connected with what calls to you from within vs. what beckons to you in the world. Here are five ways ou can tell when you are responding to what calls to you from inside. You:

- act on what matters deeply to you and fills you up
- begin to actively heal some of your empty places
- draw on your personal courage in times of fear
- speak your truth and express how you are feeling, whether in art, writing, or healthy conversation
- let your "gut" talk to you and you honor your instincts

Living in the realm of your authentic Self is freeing; you can live *in* your experience. You do not contrive it; you do not copy it from someone else. This identity is your *own* and you are living it, with truthfulness and integrity. You act intentionally on what matters to you deeply, opens you, and brings you belly-deep joy.

What yearnings lie dormant in your heart? In what way or ways do you feel called to make a difference? What stirs or is restless inside of you? What empty place calls to you to be healed? When we do not acknowledge and honor these parts of our self, we carry them around as an invisible load that drags us down or keeps us stuck.

Notice ways you live already from your center of true Self. When do you act on what you care deeply about? When do you express your feelings in healthy ways? When do you allow your inner wisdom or "knowing" to serve as your guide? And, when do you say *no* to what derails you from living your more authentic Self?

Chapter Eleven is designed to help you catch hold of and embrace your more authentic Self. Who is this integrated and balanced person waiting to live more of who you are really? What image does your heart or imagination hold of her or him? Deepen into the image, and allow the sense of your more authentic Self to evolve. Listen for this new-old voice in you.

To capture a deeper sense of your more authentic Self you will need to identify those qualities inherent in you, and you will need to imagine them in real life. You have gathered some of this information about yourself already, especially in Part Three. The Five Brief Exercises below invite you to reach into yourself and zero in more directly on your core, authentic qualities.

In Chapter Twelve, following the Five Brief Exercises, you will name the qualities you have gathered and create a personal statement of your more authentic Self. You will integrate and give life to the qualities of your true Self by giving voice lessons and identifying a symbol for this person you imagine yourself becoming.

Exercise 1. Look into Your Heart and Play with What Comes Up

 As you look out through the branches of your midlife tree, see if you can catch a glimpse of the more authentic woman or man in the distance that you imagine becoming over the years. What does your heart imagine for you? Tie a golden cord around it and let it lead you.

Your true Self is better sensed, felt, and known in your heart than it is through your mind. You are feeling the presence of this eternal and soulful part of you, when your body has a sense of being full, alive, and loving. There is a sense of clarity and "inner knowing" in the company of this place in you. Trust these feelings.

Sit back against your tree, go inward, and connect with your candid self. Let your imagination loose, and trust your instinct for play. These two elements—imagination and play—are at the center of all creative processes. When you play, your psyche moves.

Stay open to honest answers within you to cultivate a more meaningful and intimate relationship with your true Self, at the center of who you are. Trust this new voice that wants to keep you company.

Choose one of the two processes below. The first one is open-ended and the second is structured. Which one feels more "authentic" in terms of how you like to work?

Open-ended Process: Writing from Your Heart

Jot down whatever you may know already about the person you imagine becoming:

_____

_____

_____

_____

_____

Structured Process

The 10 statements below can help you clarify what truly matters to you about Who you want to become.

Fill in what comes to mind first. If you cannot think of something to write, go on to the remaining items and come back. The best approach is to work from your heart and imagination. Then, notice what they bring forward as you imagine the more authentic person in the distance. Ponder these things . . .

☑ Check the items that are especially hard for you to complete at this time.

☐ **1.** The role(s) (care giver, loyal friend, student, change agent, loving partner or spouse, active community member, leader, peace maker, grandparent, etc.) or pursuit(s) in my life that feels exciting to me is/are

_____

_____

_____

☐ **2.** A strong feeling I have about becoming more authentic is

_____

_____

_____

☐ **3.** Something I have _longed_ for in my life that I can imagine myself developing is

_____

_____

_____

☐ **4.** It would feel absolutely fantastic to me if I could make a difference in the lives of my family, friends, or others by

_____

_____

_____

☐ **5.** A shadow part in me that I imagine "making friends" with is

_____

_____

_____

☐ **6.** The kind(s) of love in my life that I imagine myself creating is/are

_____

_____

_____

☐ **7.** I see myself creating more time and space in my life for

_____

_____

_____

☐ **8.** I can see myself reviving the _____
_____ part of
me that "went underground" in earlier years, or that I "cut
off."

☐ **9.** The basic principle or ideal that I see myself working
toward, day-by-day, is

_____

_____

_____

☐ **10.** I imagine being remembered by others as someone who

_____

_____

_____

Exercise 2. Look into Your Back Pocket, Personal Notebook, Or the Back of Your Mind

In addition to what your heart and imagination have shown you, consider the information you have already gathered in your Midlife Check-In process. Look over the notes in your Back Pocket, personal notebook, or the back of your mind—wherever you may have jotted your thoughts and insights. Notice what catches your attention. What information asks to be explored? What do you want to follow up on? What will you leave in your Back Pocket for now? After taking a look at your notes, consider:

<u>What about myself do I want to:</u>

- definitely keep as is? _____
- develop or strengthen _____
- shift or change? _____
- heal or resolve? _____

  <u>Also:</u>

- What inner "rules" that I have been following do I want to break? _____
  _____

- What recommendations in the three "Where Am I?" exercises in Part Three will I follow up on?_____
  _____

Exercise 3. Possible Obstacles and Stumbling Blocks

There is a variety of ways in which we can sabotage our process of becoming more authentic. Sometimes, either consciously or unconsciously, we create personal obstacles and stumbling blocks that hold us back. They are forms of what is called emotional "resistance."

In all of our lives, there are times when we resist what we may need—or even desire—to do. We find ways to stay in our comfort zone rather than take the risk of stepping into unfamiliar territory. In your process of becoming more authentic, it is important to be aware of the ways you resist opportunities for growth. Recall from earlier chapters that increasing your consciousness and self-awareness is essential for developing a stronger connection with your true Self.

The following is a list of some of the ways people resist. They are like invisible tethers that keep us attached to our comfort zone and hold us back, often without our realizing it!

Some ways of resisting are very subtle, barely noticeable. Others are more obvious. Which of the following forms of resistance feel familiar to you? ☑ Put a check next to them.

Ways I Resist My Inner Growth

☐ Being inflexible or having excuses

☐ Not trusting or believing in myself

☐ Saying "yes," when what I really want to say is "no"

☐ Looking the other way when something or someone unknown or unfamiliar approaches

☐ Smothering an inner voice that calls to me for attention

☐ Pushing away reminders of personal loss or abandonment instead of seeking to heal my pain

☐ Pushing hard against change in my life

☐ Thinking and analyzing something to death

☐ Waiting for the "perfect" time to begin something

☐ Reacting (Giving a knee-jerk, unmanaged, automatic emotion) instead of responding (Replying consciously and thoughtfully) to a challenge

☐ Shielding myself from grief or other painful sensations

☐ Throwing a spotlight on the shortcomings I perceive in someone else, while denying my own (being critical of or blaming others)

☐ Procrastinating until I "feel like doing it"

☐ Engaging, for an extended amount of time, in an activity or pursuit that devours my time and does not fulfill me

☐ Remaining in a destructive relationship or role

☐ Holding on to resentments

☐ Feeling "less than" others

☐ Believing I cannot move forward

☐ Engaging in negative self-talk

☐ Feeling sorry for myself

☐ Letting others make decisions for me

☐ Other: _____

☐ Other: _____

<u>For each item that you checked, ask:</u>
1. What am I resisting by doing this?
2. When am I most likely to resist in this way?
3. What has my resistance led to?

Consider the personal resources you named in Part Three and the strategies you chose for managing emotional pain. How could they help you manage resistance?

℘ **NOTE:** *Managing resistance, understanding the sources of resistance, and learning skills to replace negative, automatic reactions are essential for removing emotional stumbling blocks. There are knowledgeable, skilled, and talented therapists who specialize in this work and who can support your progress toward becoming more authentic in life.*

Exercise 4. Repairs and Mendings

In previous chapters, you worked with "Holes and Empty Places" to understand the pain of unmet emotional needs that we all experience in one way or another. We human beings do not like to feel emotional pain. We think we are clever enough to outwit the underlying pain of an unmet need; we adopt strategies to avoid, hide from, bypass, cover up, or otherwise distance our self from these empty places. Yet, no matter how clever we may be in denying them, our empty places remain.

One day, we begin noticing that no matter how much "fun" we create in our life, the truth is we still are not happy. Or we notice that no matter how hard we work to build "success," we do not feel fulfilled. We discover that meanings of *things* we have accumulated, because we "had to have" them, have dissolved. We thought they would complete us—would anchor our identity—but they did not fill our empty places, after all. It turns out that they were simply "props."

Our deep emotional aches can express themselves through:
- Recurring relationship difficulties
- Hurtful emotional outbursts
- Negative beliefs about our self and the world
- Unhealthy habits and addictions
- Lack of pure, unadulterated joy
- Physical ailments

Our fundamental emotional needs include feeling safe, feeling loved, feeling that we belong, and feeling worthy. Are there any empty places or emotional wounds that might be keeping you "stuck?" How do they seem to express themselves in your life?

_____

_____

_____

Healing our emotional wounds makes it easier to center and balance ourselves. As we heal, we experience our more authentic Self.

HEALING STRATEGIES

Below is a list of strategies that many people have found to be helpful for easing and/or working through emotional pain. Look over the list. Which strategies might you use for repairs and mendings in your emotional life?

☑ **Check four or more items on the list to create your personal set of strategies for healing.**

✗ **NOTE:** *If your emotional wounds carry a history of any kind of abuse or abandonment issues, include professional support in your set of strategies. A qualified professional can help you heal these kinds of wounds at a deeper level.*

☐ Play
☐ Join a support group
☐ Read self-help books
☐ Take a personal growth class
☐ Spend personal time in nature often
☐ Share concerns with a trusted friend
☐ Write regularly in a personal journal
☐ Release tension by working with clay
☐ Paint or draw subjects of interest to you
☐ Take 5 minutes in a quiet place to just sit
☐ Use crayons to draw with abandon on inexpensive paper
☐ Go on a spiritual or other personal retreat
☐ Wrap yourself up in a warm blanket or shawl
☐ Place your hands gently over your heart space
☐ Practice quiet meditation and reflection regularly
☐ Seek professional support for doing deeper work
☐ Have a healthy eating and a regular sleeping routine
☐ Move freely to music that excites or soothes you, depending on your current feelings
☐ Seek professional support to learn how to "re-parent" yourself
☐ Other: _____

Exercise 5. My Resources for Becoming

What resources do you have within you and in your environment for becoming your more authentic Self? In this exercise, you will identify three kinds of personal resources: Golden Nuggets, Environmental Support, and Expertise.

MY GOLDEN NUGGETS

Look in your Back Pocket or personal notebook, or turn to pages 94-95 and 67 in Part Three where you listed some of your Golden Nuggets. Remember your shadow nuggets, too! Which ones do you think could help you navigate obstacles, make difficult decisions, or deal effectively with the unexpected, as you go forward?

NUGGET	HOW IT MIGHT HELP

ENVIRONMENTAL SUPPORT RESOURCES

You have resources in your personal and/or professional environment *that may be helpful in growing your authentic Self.* Look over the examples below. ☑Check the ones that are helpful to you already. Below the ones you check, name the specific resource you have:

☐ Social groups that appreciate the "real" or deeper me

_____

☐ Job or volunteer opportunities to serve individuals or the community

_____

☐ Relationships in which I can express true love and intimacy

_____

☐ Relationships which nurture my inner spirit and feed my soul

_____

☐ Groups related to healthy choices in my preferred lifestyle and
other personal practices

_____

☐ Other environmental resources I have:

_____

_____

MY EXPERTISE IN LIFE

You have looked at your golden nuggets and your environmental
support systems, two very important kinds of resources. The life skills
you have developed over the years are another valuable resource. No
doubt, you will recognize some of them on the list of seventeen skills
below. Use your life skills to enhance your authenticity in the world.

☑**Check the skills on the list which you believe are part of your "expertise" in life. Add others that you recognize in yourself.**

☐ Trusting my intuition
☐ Choosing to focus on the positives
☐ Managing my feelings in healthy ways
☐ Leading others in ways that motivate them
☐ Listening carefully to what others are saying
☐ Following through on what I say I will do
☐ Organizing details for ease of getting things done
☐ Being able to get to the core of a problem quickly
☐ Considering my options before making a decision
☐ Being true to myself, honoring personal needs and
     preferences
☐ Choosing relationships with people who inspire me
☐ Communicating with others with no hidden agendas
☐ Navigating the rough patches in life with a clear head
☐ Getting my personal needs met; asking for what I need
☐ Keeping the bigger picture in mind so I do not get lost in
     the details
☐ Managing multiple responsibilities with a sense of balance
☐ Speaking openly and calmly when I disagree with someone
☐ Asking questions to clarify something when I do not
     understand
☐ Other:_____
☐ Other: _____

Active Reflection

If you are going to bring to life your more authentic Self, it is never enough simply to label, categorize, or recognize certain events or aspects of your experience. There has be a live and aware process of reflection taking place in you to help you integrate what you have noticed or been struck by. The exercise of sitting under or leaning against your midlife tree in previous chapters was designed to help you do this. Without such conscious reflection, what you have labeled or recognized remains outside of you. It does not have true inner meaning. Only aware reflection can help you make meaning from the inside-out.

Active Reflection: Getting Ready for Your Last Midlife Check-In Exercise

Take a few minutes now to consider and reflect on what you have noticed and discovered about the more authentic person in you. This will prepare you for the next chapter and your last exercise, "I Imagine Myself Becoming Someone Who . . . ."

Ask Yourself:

"Who is this more authentic Self in me? What matters most to me in my heart? What qualities are most consistent in this person I seek to become?"

These qualities are reflections of what your more authentic Self believes about you and how to manage needs, feelings and behaviors.

Where to Look for Ideas:

Look through your responses to the five exercises above and to the following exercises in the previous chapter:

- My Personal Integration: Where Am I?
- Ten Below: Digging Deeper
- Golden Nuggets: Unseen Assets
- Traits Associated with Being "Real"
- Assessing Your Authenticity

Make note of the core qualities you want to develop or enhance. In addition, note the shadow parts you plan to acknowledge, the empty places you want to heal, and the defensive behaviors you would like to let go of, as you live more and more of your true Self. Doing so will definitely help you become the more authentic person you can imagine.

<u>Core qualities to develop or enhance in myself:</u>

<u>Shadow parts to acknowledge:</u>

<u>Empty places to heal:</u>

<u>Defensive behaviors to let go of:</u>

<u>FEELINGS GAUGE:</u>
WHAT AM I FEELING, *RIGHT NOW*?

<u>Circle the number on the scale</u> below that best describes how you are feeling *right now, in this very moment*. **0** represents the calmest feeling state and **10** represents the most upset feeling state. Descriptions of associated body sensations are shown at each extreme to help you gauge where your feelings are *in this moment*.

0 . . .1 . . .2 . . .3 . . .4 . . .5 . . .6 . . .7 . . .8 . . .9 . . .10

Clear ....Confused
Centered..Scattered
Relaxed, Still..Tense, Agitated
Nonjudgmental....................................Reactive, Critical
Slow deep breathing...........................Rapid breathing
Resting pulse rate................................Fast pulse
In total peace.......................................On high alert

21 WAYS I CAN TAKE CARE OF MYSELF
RIGHT NOW

It is important to have simple and effective ways to manage your tension and uncomfortable feelings in the moment. Below are 21 ideas. Using these can help you move quickly toward a more relaxed and balanced state of being.

☑ Check the ones you like most:

☐ Breathe deeply and slowly

☐ Move freely to music

☐ Stand, stretch, walk around

☐ Do 10-20 jumping jacks

☐ Bend gently side to side, then forward slightly
☐ Beat a drum

☐ Light a candle and be with its light for a few minutes

☐ Hold or stroke my pet
☐ Move to a different space

☐ Watch a funny movie

☐ Climb into my midlife tree

☐ Be in nature near flowers, trees, water, soothing views

☐ Hug myself and breathe

☐ Ring my singing bowl

☐ Speak with a trusted friend

☐ Drink a warm beverage such as herbal tea, milk, soup
☐ Laugh out loud

☐ Shift my body position and breathe deeply

☐ Place my hands over my heart
☐ Focus on an inspiring image

☐ Make a positive statement about myself

Midlife Glossary:
Check Out These Words

Below is a list of glossary words you may wish to explore in relation to this chapter. ☑Put a check by any that "call" to you, and find their meanings in the Midlife Glossary. How might the words relate to *the more authentic person you imagine yourself becoming?*

☐ authentic nature   ☐ mortality

☐ becoming   ☐ self-assessment

☐ calling   ☐ threshold

☐ choice point   ☐ wholeheartedness

☐ courage   ☐ wisdom

☐ healing

Sitting and Reflecting Under My Midlife Tree

"In search of my mother's garden I found my own."
Alice Walker

• Sit and Reflect

What captured my attention most?
What puzzled or concerned me?
What do I want to explore further?
How can the more authentic person I imagine
myself becoming affect my life today?

Sit and Reflect

Take a few moments now to climb down from your personal tree of midlife to sit under it and reflect actively on the question, "Who is the more authentic person I imagine myself becoming?" When you are in a comfortable spot, take a s-l-o-w relaxation belly breath in; let it out s-l-o-w-l-y.

Open to a few quiet moments with yourself, with no expectations. Consider the work you have done with the Five Brief Exercises and ask yourself the four questions listed above. What colors and patterns can you imagine the Seven Threads of Becoming weaving in you, as you live your more authentic Self?

In this space of inner conversation insights may grab your attention, questions may surface, or ideas for personal actions may materialize. Who knows? Just relax for a few minutes in your own company under the canopy of your midlife tree. Just be . . .

Chapter Twelve

"I Imagine Myself
Becoming Someone Who . . ."

> *"I am not afraid—I was born to do this."*
> Joan of Arc

Write specific ideas in the ten categories below to complete the statement,
"I imagine myself becoming someone who..."

. . .Has A Strong, Positive Self-Concept.

I believe I

_____

_____

_____

. . .Knows and Acts on What Matters Deeply.

I care deeply about or am strongly committed to

_____

_____

_____

. . .Is Conscious of Feelings and Behaviors and Manages Them in Healthy Ways.

I manage my feelings and behaviors

_____

_____

_____

. . .Is Proactive in Getting Personal Needs Met.

I get my personal needs met by

_____

_____

_____

. . .Works to Heal Empty Places.

I am healing

_____

_____

_____

. . .Taps into Creative Energies.

I express my creative energy with

_____

_____

_____

. . .Pays Attention to Inner "Knowing."

I connect with my inner wisdom by

_____

_____

_____

. . .Lets Go of What No Longer "Fits."

I am letting go of (defenses, resentments, old beliefs, roles, etc.)

_____

_____

_____

. . .Is Playful.

My playful self emerges when I

_____

_____

_____

. . .Laughs Wholeheartedly.

I am moved to laugh wholeheartedly when

_____

_____

_____

Voice Lessons

When we say *aloud* something we are feeling, something we believe, or something that matters to us, we breathe life into it; we give it voice. You have created a description of a more authentic person you imagine becoming. Now, it is time to give this person voice and energy!

Directions:

1. <u>Read to yourself</u> exactly what you wrote in each section of "I Am Becoming Someone Who . . ." How do you *feel* as you read this?

2. Now, <u>stand up</u> and read it a second time. <u>Use your voice</u> to give it life. Anchor yourself where you are standing. Read it aloud in a way that feels solid and credible to you.

3. Continue practicing in this way until you feel *very* comfortable in voice and posture as you make your statements.
   Notice: Do your voice and body posture reflect each other? (Sometimes it helps to stand in front of a mirror and do this.)

4. Read the statements to your reflection in the mirror a few times.

5. Now, imagine yourself making these statements to a group of people. Read them aloud in the strongest, most believable voice you have! Notice how you are feeling inside as you do.

If you notice that something you wrote does not feel comfortable when you say it aloud, wonder about it . . . Do you need to change it in some way? Do the words fit for who you imagine yourself becoming? Play with your ideas.

Practice this voice lesson daily during the coming days and weeks. Look for opportunities to "try on" ways of being more of your true Self. Listen for this person in your Self-talk.

A Symbol of My True Self

In Part Three you identified a symbol to represent:

Who I have been: _____
                     (Name of the symbol or image)

Who I am now: _____
                     (Name of the symbol or image)

Who I am *really*: _____
                     (Name of the symbol or image)

What symbol might represent
the more authentic person you imagine becoming?

Perhaps it is a blend of the first three symbols you chose in Part Three? Maybe it is very much like one of them? Or, it may be that you need a completely different symbol or image for her. If that is the case, consider looking for an idea or a combination of ideas in "Appendix C: Symbols of the Self."

Describe the symbol you have chosen in the spaces below:

_____

_____

_____

_____

Climb Back Up Into Your Tree . . .

Feel the support of your tree and how it embraces you. Let the breezes move around you, blow through your hair, and refresh you. What is next for you on your journey of becoming more authentic? Use the list below for some ideas and check any that call to you *now*:

☐ Use positive images or inspiring examples to motivate me
☐ Be selective about how, when, and where I will invest my time, energy, and other personal resources
☐ Learn new skills or train in a new field
☐ Pay attention to my self-talk and how I validate myself or put myself down
☐ Connect with people who inspire and motivate me
☐ Learn healthy ways to respond to my feelings
☐ Make notes about my dreams and seek professional help to understand them
☐ Notice the images, music, words that "move" me in comfortable and uncomfortable ways
☐ Identify a relationship I want to reconcile, forgive, or let go of
☐ Explore interests that feed my soul
☐ Let go of what no longer represents who I am
☐ Acknowledge my shadow
☐ Get to know the ways my body talks to me in situations of pleasure and stress
☐ Connect with the untapped energy hidden in me through quiet and solitude, journaling, inspirational reading, art

THE CALL

The Midlife Check-In process has asked you to meet yourself head-on, with a call to become more who you are than you have ever been. You have given honest answers to some tough questions—required work for becoming more of who you really are and for being at home in your own skin.

Know that you have done important work! You have become more conscious of Who you are. You have learned ways to deepen connection with your true Self. You have dared to imagine the more authentic person you want to become . . .

My greatest hope is that your process has been meaningful for you and that it has increased and deepened Self-awareness and understanding. Perhaps it has created in you a deeper appreciation for the mystery of Who you are *really*. I also hope it has brought home to you the courage and strength you have drawn from in your life.

You are breathing life into a conscious vision of your true Self. To grow into this vision in the midst of a beckoning world is a delicate balancing act, which requires your ongoing attention and renewed commitment.

Continue your journey inward. Allow connection with your deeper Self to evolve. Nature's intention for you is to live your wholeness, as in a blooming tulip or a fully-grown tree—the beautiful outcome of an inner journey that takes place over time. ༄༅

Afterword

As you move through these years and beyond, remember that your tree is wise. Your tree speaks to you. Listen with your soul ear.

⚙

"Be like a tree!
Know who you are. Stand firm and beautiful in your knowing. Interact with the world in life-giving ways.

Stand firm in your place between earth and sky, and be flexible. Let breezes, winds, and gales pass through, as they will. Remain who you are; be beautiful in your natural presence.

Draw up nourishment and insights from lessons learned, skills mastered, people and things lost—the composting and rooting of life experiences. Draw nourishment from the trust and courage that have kept you growing. Draw up your dreams into consciousness and encourage new growth.

Draw down wonder, awe, and illumination from the Mystery above. Let them stir up new energy in you and in your imagination.

Settle into your darkest hours. Await what is trying to come. Listen, as something deeper and wiser stirs in you. Alone, in the dark of night, be still. Let the knowing within you emerge from the secrets at the center of your being.

Be still in the knowing of who you are.
Be like a tree and say I am!"

⚙

MarthaElin Mountain, 2012
Midlife Check-In: Who Am I *Really*?

ACKNOWLEDGEMENTS

The creation of Midlife Check-In has been an organic process. It has grown from its initial draft as a workbook through inspired stages and interactions with a variety of people and resources.

Many supportive and knowledgeable individuals helped me give form to this book. They are mental health professionals, good friends, colleagues, and fellow travelers who served as sounding boards and helpful critics. I want to acknowledge, in particular, my late dear friend and colleague, Barbara B. Nelson, M.A., MFT, whose sage suggestions at the inception of my project and during many of the months that followed, unblocked the logjams of my writer's mind and freed my muse with a flood of ideas and inspirations. I have dedicated Midlife Check-In to her.

As my ideas evolved, my Jungian study group friends and colleagues were generous with their support, expertise, and thoughtful feedback. My heartfelt thanks to Judy, Andrea, Barbara, Eileen, Pat, and Lydia. No doubt, you will recognize some of your contributions to this book.

Linda Coyne, M.A. brought her keen mind and sharp eye to important details of the book's infrastructure. Her incisive feedback was invaluable for increasing the visual and user-friendly appeal of the content, as well. Victoria Singer, Ph.D. offered sensitive descriptions of the deeper Self, which helped me find words to convey the mystery of this part in us. Lydia Davis, MFT gave various versions of the developing manuscript a thoughtful, thorough, and constructive reading. Her feedback was creative and inspiring.

Central to the evolution of Midlife Check-In, and to whom I am very grateful, are my clients—individuals and couples who have shared stories with me about their journeys in life and midlife years. They have asked heartfelt questions and revealed deep concerns, inner struggles, and personal truths. I am grateful for their trust and openness.

The ten participants in my first "Midlife Check-In for Proactive Women" group deserve a special nod of appreciation. They gave some of the exercises a trial run and participated enthusiastically in the various group processes. Their personal stories and candid feedback were invaluable in helping me conceptualize and create meaningful and useful material for this book.

I want to extend special appreciation to the twenty-one "full-moon" women in their 70s, 80s, and 90s, who provided personal and valuable background information for this book. They contributed reflections about their own midlife years, as well as specific advice for the midlife women who will read this book. When quoting a full-moon woman, I have used her actual name, with permission, or the pseudonym she chose.

My sincere gratitude goes to the professionals, whose names appear on the first pages of the book, for their thoughtful, generous, and enthusiastic advance praise.

Of critical importance to any manuscript are the skills of an adept and conscientious editor. I want to thank CatherineRose Mountain who reviewed my work with care and editorial authority. Her attention to the manuscript was skillful, efficient, and spot-on. She made insightful suggestions of words and phrasing to increase readability and consistency, without compromising the integrity of my ideas and intended meanings.

The contributions numerous authors have made to the literature about midlife provided important facts, insights, and inspiration as I prepared to write this book. I would like to acknowledge particular authors. Their approaches to the subject differ, and we may resonate more with one than another, but in every case they have brightened the light on the subject and have directed it in and around the deeper nooks and crannies of who we are really and are meant to become. They are scholars and beacons in the field of depth psychology and personal transformation: J.S. Bolen, J. Borysenko, E.F. Edinger, C.P. Estes, J. Hillman, J. Hollis, R.A. Johnson, C.G. Jung, R.N. Remen, M. Stein, D. Winnicott, and M. Woodman.

A special thank you to Jean Shinoda Bolen for her book Like a Tree that inspired my idea for creating the Tree of Midlife and using it as a symbol and metaphor within the Midlife Check-In process.

Certain authors were very helpful in bringing me up to date with brain research, especially with regard to the middle-aged and older brain. The following authors contributed greatly to my understanding: G. Cohen, N. Doidge, D.J. Siegel, and B. Strauch.

Endeavors such as this one are inspired very often by examples of others. The personal example, creative influence, and gentle encouragement of Marcelle Vernazza, over the years, spurred my desire to "write a book someday." Thank you, Mom, for the vision...

A very important person, without whom I would not have been able to complete this project, is my husband. He has offered the kinds of support that enable a writing spouse to thrive in her process: delicious and healthy home-cooked meals, acceptance of my need to "burrow into" my writing mode, thoughtful suggestions of midlife films to view, patience with a dining room table camouflaged by manuscript pages, and many encouraging hugs. This book has been a labor of love that might have taken me several more years to birth were it not for his loving support.

MarthaElin Mountain
Midlife Check-In, 2012

 Clinician, author, speaker, educator— MarthaElin Mountain, Ed.D., M.A., MFT is a Licensed Marriage and Family Therapist and a Jungian-based psychotherapist. Her practice focuses on emotional change in individuals and couples and on personal transformation and balance in midlife and beyond. Brain-mind-body-spirit informs her practice, especially in regard to mood and motivation, past trauma, unresolved inner conflicts, creativity, performance, and aging.

Dr. Mountain draws on nearly 40 years of acquired expertise and varied experience in her Psychology and Education careers. In recent years, she has designed and led several experiential, thought-provoking programs for midlife travelers and elders, including "Circle of Wisdom," "Exploring What Makes Life Meaningful," "Aging Well and Wisely," and "Midlife Check-In for Proactive Women." She has also initiated and implemented programs to include mental health support services within early childhood and senior living settings.

MarthaElin Mountain's practice includes a specialization in the unique social-emotional risks and diagnostic challenges of giftedness. She is a community resource for gifted adults, children, and families, and for clinicians and schools.

Dr. Mountain earned her graduate degrees in Education, Organizational Behavior, Qualitative Evaluation, and Psychology from Stanford; U.C., Berkeley; and Chapman Universities. Her research and work in child and adult goal setting behaviors have appeared in professional publications and the Guidance Channel E-zine.

MarthaElin Mountain is a seasoned midlife traveler; she has witnessed the search for identity, meaning, and purpose from a front-row seat. Tucked into her back pocket is her cherished notebook of collected wisdom, wonderings, and lessons learned, with her pencil always ready for new entries! MarthaElin and her husband live on California's Central Coast, where she maintains a private practice and facilitates the group experience, "Midlife Check-In for Proactive Women."

For more information, you may contact the author at:
www.drmarthaelin.com
www.therapyforgifted.com

More Support?

It is important to continue this personal work, whether alone, with a group, and/or with professional support. If you feel that what you have learned about yourself in your Midlife Check-In experience has been valuable, and you believe that you could benefit from additional help, you may want to consider working with others, such as a group or a therapist.

Groups

Working with like-minded souls in workshops or support groups can eliminate feelings of isolation in your quest to develop your true Self. It can also help you challenge your ego's patterns of resistance to becoming more authentic. Confronting such tendencies may mean setting priorities that differ from those held by your family, friends, and colleagues—something that is hard to do alone.

Therapist

Therapy is an opportunity to gain deeper insight into yourself and to make choices and changes for a more authentic and satisfying life. You may want to consider working with a therapist who specializes in depth work to help you explore and heal the empty places in you. A skilled therapist can help you develop the qualities and practices of the more authentic person you imagine becoming.

A book can provide some background, suggest ways of working toward a more authentic life, and give guidelines for the journey. It cannot, however, replace personal contact with others or the feedback of a professional. I encourage you to make the choices that support you and your vision.

Therapist's Guide

The tools and materials in Midlife Check-In can help you:

- Assess clients during the initial and later phases of therapy
- Build conversation around sensitive issues
- Move a client into the space of inner work
- Normalize experiences common to midlife shifts
- Zero in on underlying issues and concerns
- Understand a client's self-concept
- Show clients the ways we defend ourselves and resist change
- Encourage healthy life skills practices
- Explain abstract concepts, such as "conscious," "ego," "unconscious," "authenticity," "Self," "shadow," "symbol," "wholeness"
- Facilitate a client's connection with empty places calling for emotional or spiritual healing
- Identify and explore clients' existential questions
- Include periods of quiet and reflection during sessions
- Understand a client's family-of-origin history
- Educate clients about the facts and myths concerning midlife
- Increase client awareness of inner resources

Introduction

Midlife Check-In is a practical resource and reference for your work with clients in midlife and beyond—no matter what theoretical orientation(s) you favor. <u>The Guide is organized in three sections:</u>

- **<u>Section One:</u>**
Ways to Use Midlife Check-In
- **<u>Section Two:</u>**
Handy Lists of Exercises for Specific Purposes
- **<u>Section Three:</u>**
Recommended Resources

With more than seventy exercises, self-assessment tools, and factual references at your disposal you have a variety of options to choose from for any of several purposes in your work.

An underlying purpose of this practical resource is to help readers, and your clients, develop a hopeful perspective and a proactive stance in their midlife years and beyond. It encourages them to take the reins of their journey. I hope that, as a therapist, you will find Midlife Check-In to be a unique and useful clinical resource for understanding the many transformative aspects of the midlife experience, for educating your clients, and for helping them deepen their sense of Self as they work through their presenting and underlying issues.

> **<u>A Note to Life Coaches:</u>** *If you are a Life Coach, you will find that many of the exercises and resources in Midlife Check-In can be excellent tools in your work. In the contexts of personal therapy and depth work, and interventions related to emotional and diagnostic needs, the use of an exercise is limited to the scope of practice of a licensed mental health practitioner. As you know, it is always important to make this distinction when deciding how you will use a Midlife Check-In exercise.*

☒**NOTE:** As the therapist, you are always in charge of what you do and when, and which tools or materials suit your client's needs and readiness, and the treatment plan. This Guide is intended only as a helpful reference to Midlife Check-In materials and their possible uses for therapy purposes. It is not a prescription for your therapy approach or decisions.

Section One: Ways to Use Midlife Check-In

• **Individuals and Groups**
• **Sequential or Random Use**
• **Focusing on the Three Core Questions of Midlife**

Individuals and Groups

Depending on the goals of therapy, your theoretical approach, and your immediate purpose, you can use the exercises and tools in Midlife Check-In as stand-alone prompts and assessments or to create your own process with individuals and with groups.

Individuals: The practical information and numerous self-assessment exercises can provide you and your clients with helpful feedback and meaningful points for discussion. With individuals, you can use Midlife Check-In as an integral part of the therapy process, as a recommended client resource, or as a handy reference and source of clinical materials.

A client may decide to use Midlife Check-In while working with you in therapy or counseling. In this case, I recommend that you invite her or him to check in and share some questions and insights from the Check-In process. You may also want to point your client toward particular exercises related to your work with her. It helps to keep you on the "same page," strengthen the therapist-client connection, and develop your client's ownership of the process.

Groups: The information, tools, and exercises in this book can be adapted easily for use with groups. With a therapy group, you can use Midlife Check-In materials to focus on specific kinds of experiences (self-assessment, education, life skills practice, reflection), on the positives in clients' lives, and on nonverbal ways to express personal information (art, movement, symbols).

Midlife Check-In materials can help a group to explore symptoms of anxiety and depression, what is normal or not, and to move into the deeper places of one's past and present experiences. Depending on the level of trust and safety the group has developed exercises may be done in dyads or partners.

Midlife Check-In is also an ideal book for an educational group focused on the meaning of midlife, the core questions, and healthy strategies for managing their lives. Words that you or group members select from the Midlife Glossary are an easy way to prompt discussions about their connections with midlife and personal experiences.

Sequential or Random Use

When followed sequentially, Midlife Check-In progresses from a more concrete level of self-assessment and -observation toward a deepening inner-directed experience of self-awareness. In the course of the process, Midlife Check-In touches base with nearly every possible concern or issue that women and men can encounter in their midlife years; it provides a multitude of options for exploring them, in a gently guided and thoughtful process.

Typically, our clients come to us with a concern or issue that is current; they want help with something now. Engaging your client with some of the information and exercises in Chapter Nine, *Who Am I Now?*, can help her move into the initial phase of therapy and, at the same time, provide you with more varied and useful self-report information. Exercises like "My Golden Nuggets: Hidden Assets," "My Identity in the Present," "What Brings Me Joy," and "A Symbol of Who I Am Now" can engage a client in unexpected ways. Such exercises can also provide helpful direction for therapy work.

I have found that using Midlife Check-In exercises at appropriate points in time can lead clients to connect with important issues that they may not have addressed earlier because they were uncomfortable speaking about them, had not been conscious of them, or because other issues had felt more urgent.

Focusing on the Three Core Questions of Midlife

Each of the three chapters in Part Three focuses on one of the core questions of midlife and beyond. They include relevant exercises and information, with opportunities to reflect. Here are three ways you might want to use these chapters or parts of them with clients:

1. As part of your early assessment and information-gathering
2. To support a therapy focus on the past, present, or future aspects of a client's life
3. To develop and deepen the client's awareness of the larger question(s), or core question, behind a presenting concern.

Most of the concerns clients bring to therapy or counseling in their midlife years are related to one or more of the three core questions: *"Who have I been?" "Who am I now?" "Who am I—really?"* When you recognize the core question underlying your client's immediate concern, you position yourself to bring a larger and deeper focus to the work with a client. You keep the bigger picture in mind, which gives you a context for the work. Your awareness of an underlying question can help you to develop a treatment plan for some clients that:

- prepares the client to address the larger question,
- helps the client address her immediate concern *and* relate it to the larger question,
- includes interventions for deepening self-awareness, and
- expands the meaning of her work in therapy.

The following list relates typical concerns of midlife clients to the three core questions.

Concerns Related to "Who Have I Been?"

"Why didn't I see this coming? Why am I so blind?"

"Painful memories just keep coming up; they get in the way. How can I move on?"

"I've been through three marriages, and I always end up leaving. Why can't I find someone, love him/her, and stay?"

"I feel stuck. Something is holding me back; I just can't seem to move forward with my life."

"For years, I've just kept busy and avoided getting too close to anyone."

"It's hard for me to really *feel* anything."

"I feel a kind of sadness inside of me most of the time, and I don't know why. It's not that I have anything to be unhappy about, really. My life is going ok, but I'm just not that excited about things."

Concerns Related to "Who Am I Now?"

"I think I'm falling out of love with my partner. It feels like the person I am now is different from the person I was when we first got together."

"The things that have really mattered to me for many years don't seem to matter so much anymore."

"I've spent most of my life taking care of everybody else; now I want to take care of *me*. Is this ok?"

"Right now, I'm not sure just where I'm supposed to focus my attention: my parents are needing me more, my kids have their issues, and I'm trying to keep up with new challenges at work. I don't know if I can manage all of this and be sane!"

"I thought I had things pretty well figured out; life seemed to be working. Now, it feels as if my family is turning against me."

"I kind of feel like I'm living two lives—but the truth is that neither one really feels like 'me'."

"Ok, now what? My kids are moving out. I want to do something different, but I don't have a clue!"

"There doesn't seem to be any room in my life for my *real* interests or passions."

"How do I cope with body changes, family changes, and just feeling 'old'?"

Concerns Related to "Who Am I—*Really*?"

"I want to be more myself—to be *real* in how I live my life."

"It feels like there's something missing in my life."

"How can I get off the treadmill and still feel successful?"

"What the heck have I been *do*ing with my life? I need to make some changes . . ."

"How do I get away from the toxic influences in my life? My spirit is dying a slow death."

"I'm feeling anxious about the next few years of my life. I've made so many mistakes, bad choices. I want to make up for them in the time I have left, but I'm not sure if that's possible."

"After all is said and done, I don't really feel my life has much meaning for me."

> ## Section Two: Handy Lists of
> ## Exercises for Specific Purposes
>
> ### 1. Each Exercise and Its Clinical Purpose
> ### 2. The Initial Phase of Therapy
> ### 3. Tracking Client Progress
> ### 4. Educating Clients
> ### 5. Deepening Client Self-Awareness
> ### 6. Life Review with Full-Moon Clients

1. Each Exercise and Its Clinical Purpose

The list that follows will help you find exercises and tools that are appropriate for the purpose you have in mind: Assessment, Information or Reference, Life Skill Practice, Reflection.

Purpose Key:
     A = Assessment
     I/R = Information, Reference
     LS = Life Skill Practice
     R = Reflection

Exercise	A	I/R	LS	R
PART ONE				
Chapter One				
Tools	X			
Personal Choices	X			
Chapter Two				
What Are You Feeling in This Moment?			X	
Feelings Gauge©		X		X
21 Ways I Can Take Care of Myself Right Now			X	

Exercise	A	I/R	LS	R

PART TWO

Chapter Three

The Midlife Checklist©	X			

Chapter Four

Which Phase(s) of Midlife Am I in Now?		X		
Which Threads of Becoming Do My Answers Focus on Most?	X			
Focus on One of My Top Threads of Becoming				X

Chapter Five

The Three Midlife Phases: Their Moons, Meanings, Murmurings, Movement		X		
Bird's-Eye View of Shifts and Overlaps	X	X		

Chapter Six

What Comes Up Often in Midlife	X	X		

Chapter Seven

But Wait! What About the Full Moon?		X		

PART THREE

Chapter Eight

Getting Started: Charting Your Pre-Midlife Years				X
A Meaningful Year in My Past				X
My Golden Nuggets: Gifts from My Pre-Midlife Years	X			X
My Story: Capturing a Positive Experience From My Past				X
My Identity in the Past	X			X
My Identity: Assumed or Real?	X			
A Symbol of Who I Have Been	X			X
Ten Below	X			X
Notice and Reflect				X
Holes and Empty Places: Unmet Needs From My Past	X	X		

Exercise	A	I/R	LS	R
Negative Beliefs and Self-Doubts	X			
Five Unhealthy Strategies We May Adopt in Order to Get Our Emotional Needs Met		X		
Four Unhealthy Strategies We May Use in Order to Feel Safe		X		
Where Am I?	X	X		
Feelings Gauge				X
21 Ways I Can Take Care of Myself Right Now			X	
Midlife Glossary: Check Out These Words		X		
Sit and Reflect				X
Back Pocket		X		X
Chapter Nine				
My Golden Nuggets: Hidden Assets	X			X
My Story: Rescripting a Challenging Experience			X	X
Baby Boomer or Generation X-er?	X			X
My Identity in the Present	X			
What Brings Me Joy?	X			X
A Symbol of Who I Am Now	X			X
Ten Below	X			X
Notice and Reflect				X
Holes and Empty Places: Portals to Opportunity	X	X		
Where Am I?	X	X		
Feelings Gauge©				X
21 Ways I Can Take Care of Myself Right Now©			X	
Midlife Glossary: Check Out These Words		X		
Lean Back and Reflect				X
Back Pocket		X		X
Chapter Ten				
The "You" Behind Your Eyes			X	X
Traits Associated with Being Real	X			
My Personal Integration: Where Am I?	X	X		X
Practice with Visualization			X	
Practice with Wondering			X	

Exercise	A	I/R	LS	R
Some of My Unseen Nuggets	X			
Shadow Nuggets	X			
My Own Shifts	X		X	
Are Any of These False Assumptions Mine?	X			
A Symbol of Who I Am—*Really*	X			X
Ten Below	X			X
Notice and Reflect				X
Defenses	X		X	
My Own Repeated Encounter	X			
Assessing Your Authenticity	X			
Where Am I?	X	X		
Feelings Gauge©				X
21 Ways I Can Take Care of Myself Right Now ©			X	
Midlife Glossary: Check Out These Words		X		
Sit and Reflect				X
Back Pocket		X		X

PART FOUR

Chapter Eleven

	A	I/R	LS	R
Next Steps in Becoming				X
Look into Your Heart and Play with What Comes Up			X	
Look into Your Back Pocket, Personal Notebook, or the Back of Your Mind				X
Possible Obstacles and Stumbling Blocks: Ways I Resist My Inner Growth	X	X		
Healing Strategies			X	
My Resources for Becoming:				
My Golden Nuggets	X			
Environmental Support Resources	X			
My Expertise in Life	X			
Getting Ready for Your Last Midlife				
Check-In Exercise	X			X

Exercise	A	I/R	LS	R
What Have You Noticed and Discovered?			X	X
Feelings Gauge ©				X
21 Ways I Can Take Care of Myself Right Now			X	
Midlife Glossary: Check Out These Words		X		
Sit and Reflect	X			X
Chapter Twelve				
I Imagine Myself Becoming Someone Who . . .	X		X	
Voice Lessons			X	
A Symbol of My True Self	X			X
Climb Back Up into Your Tree	X		X	
AFTERWORD				X
APPENDICES				
Appendix A: What's Normal? What's Not?	X	X		
Appendix B: Healthy and Unhealthy				
Responses to Midlife		X		
Appendix C: Symbols of the Self	X	X		
MIDLIFE GLOSSARY		X		
BIBLIOGRAPHY		X		
INDEX		X		
BACK POCKET	X	X	X	X

2. Initial Phase of Therapy

Some of the Midlife Check-In exercises are especially useful during the initial phase of therapy when you and your client are building trust and gathering helpful information for your work together. Some tools are also helpful for clients to use during a crisis situation.

As stated earlier, you are always in charge of what you do and when, and which tools or materials suit your client's needs and readiness, and the treatment plan. The listed exercises that follow are suggestions only. You may want to modify an exercise or use it purely for building conversation with your client, instead of having the client complete it independently.

Patience may be your guideword, if your client does not or cannot follow through with completing an exercise. There may be apprehension about the feelings it may bring up, the time period it focuses on, or the topic it relates to.

After you and your client have processed her experience with a given exercise, you may want to continue with another or a group of exercises. For example, if your focus is on helping your client to explore her "story" in a focused way, she may benefit from completing the "My Story" exercise in each chapter of Part Three.

If your purpose is to help your client identify "unfinished business" in his life, you might suggest the "Ten Below" exercise found in each chapter of Part Three as a way of getting started.

Exercise	**Where You Can Find I**
• What Are You Feeling in This Moment?	Chapter Two
• Feelings Gauge ©	
• 21 Ways I Can Take Care of Myself in This Moment ©	
• The Midlife Checklist©	Chapter Three
• What Comes Up Often in Midlife	Chapter Six
• Getting Started: Charting Your Pre-Midlife Years	Chapter Eight

Exercise	**Where You Can Find I**
• A Meaningful Year in My Past	
• My Golden Nuggets: Gifts from My Pre-Midlife Years	
• My Story: Capturing a Positive Experience from My Past	
• Negative Beliefs and Self-Doubts	
• Baby Boomer or Generation X-er?	Chapter Nine
• What Brings Me Joy?	
• My Own Shifts	Chapter Ten
• Possible Obstacles and Stumbling Blocks:	Chapter Eleven
Ways I Resist My Inner Growth	
(Parts of "My Resources for Becoming"):	Chapter Eleven
• Healing Strategies	
• Environmental Support Resources	
• My Expertise in Life	
• What's Normal" What's Not?	Appendix A
(Anxiety and Depression in Midlife)	
• Healthy and Unhealthy Responses to Midlife	Appendix B

3. Tracking Client Progress

Many of the exercises cross-referenced with "A" (Assessment) in the first list can be useful for tracking a client's short-term or longer-term progress with a specific goal or challenge. You can use many of the exercises as pre-post assessments.

Exercise	**Where You Can Find It**
• Feelings Gauge ©	Chapter Two
• Which Threads of Becoming Do My Answers Focus on Most?	Chapter Four
• What Comes Up Often in Midlife?	Chapter Six
• Where Am I?	Chapters Eight, Nine, Ten
• Ten Below (specific items your client checked)	
• Traits Associated with Being Real	Chapter Ten
• My Personal Integration: Where Am I?	
• My Own Repeated Encounter	
• Possible Obstacles and Stumbling Blocks:	Chapter Eleven
Ways I Resist My Inner Growth	
• What's Normal? What's Not? ©	Appendix A
• Healthy and Unhealthy Responses to Midlife	Appendix B

4. Educating Clients:

The following exercises and tools are useful for normalizing certain experiences or concerns in midlife and for helping clients understand and relate to particular concepts and life practices.

Exercise	**Where You Can Find It**
• What Are You Feeling in This Moment?	Chapter Two
• Feelings Gauge ©	
• 21 Ways I Can Take Care of Myself Right Now ©	
• The Three Midlife Phases: Their Moons, Meanings, Murmurings, Movement	Chapter Five

Exercise	**Where You Can Find It**
• Bird's-Eye View of Shifts and Overlaps	
• What Comes Up Often in Midlife	Chapter Six
• Five Unhealthy Strategies We May Adopt in Order to Get Our Emotional Needs Met	Chapter Eight
• Four Unhealthy Strategies We May Use in Order to Feel Safe	Chapter Eight
• My Story: Rescripting a Challenging Experience	Chapter Nine
• Holes and Empty Places: Portals to Opportunity	
• Traits Associated with Being Real	Chapter Ten
• Practice with Visualization	
• Practice with Wondering	
• Shadow Nuggets	
• Healing Strategies	Chapter Eleven
• Voice Lessons	Chapter Twelve
• What's Normal? What's Not?	Appendix A
• Healthy and Unhealthy Responses to Midlife	Appendix B
• Symbols of the Self	Appendix C
• Extended Learning	Midlife Glossary
	Bibliography

5. Deepening Client Self-Awareness

You may find the following exercises and tools useful for helping clients develop a deeper connection with themselves, become more conscious of thoughts and behaviors, and increase Self awareness.

Exercise	Where You Can Find It
• Feelings Gauge ©	Chapters Two, Eight, Nine, Ten, Eleven
• What Comes Up Often in Midlife	Chapter Six
• My Identity in the Past	Chapter Eight
• My Identity: Assumed of Real	
• A Symbol of Who I Have Been	Chapter Eight
• Ten Below	Chapters Eight, Nine, Ten
• Holes and Empty Places: Unmet Needs from My Past	Chapter Eight
• Where Am I?	Chapters Eight, Nine, Ten
• (Sitting) Under My Midlife Tree	Chapters Eight, Nine, Ten
• What Brings Me Joy?	Chapter Nine
• A Symbol of Who I Am Now	
• Holes and Empty Places: Portals to Opportunity	
• The "You" Behind Your Eyes	Chapter Ten
• My Personal Integration: Where Am I?	
• Practice with Visualization	
• Practice with Wondering	
• Some of My Unseen Nuggets	
• Shadow Nuggets	
• My Own Shifts	
• Are Any of These False Assumptions Mine?	
• A Symbol of Who I Am—*Really*	

Exercise	**Where You Can Find It**
• Defenses	
• My Own Repeated Encounter	
• Assessing Your Authenticity	
• Look into Your Heart and Play with What Comes Up	Chapter Eleven
• Possible Obstacles and Stumbling Blocks: Ways I Resist My Inner Growth	
• I Imagine Myself Becoming Someone Who . . .	Chapter Twelve
• Voice Lessons	
• A Symbol of My True Self	

6. Life Review with Full-Moon Clients

Many of the Midlife Check-In exercises can be very helpful if you are working with older clients, especially if you are working in a life review process. The exercises can provide an avenue or structure for looking back.

The purpose of a life review is to acquire insight and clarity about one's lifetime in order to make sense of it—in order to give it meaning. Some individuals intend for a life review process to be an intrapersonal exploration only. Others want to leave a legacy, a personal story or, what I call, a "wisdom gift" for the younger generation in their family. They want to draw from their life review and share personal anecdotes, lessons learned, and helpful information.

If an older client chooses to delve *deeply* into his or her history of personal development, consider using the "Ten Below" exercises or parts of them. Also, you might find the Back Pocket (or a similar "container" that you create yourself) to be a useful tool for tracking and organizing your client's information during a life review process. As always, the choices are yours.

The following two books about the life review process are excellent professional references, should you wish to explore this specialized work in more detail:

Haight, Barbara and Barrett S. Haight. *The Handbook of Structured Life Review*. Baltimore: Health Professions Press, 2007.

Kunz, John and Florence Soltys. *Transformational Reminiscence: Life Story Work*. New York: Springer Publishing Co., LLC, 2007.

Exercise to Use with Life Review	Where You Can Find It
• Getting Started: Charting Your Pre-Midlife Years *(Modify this to suit timeframe.)*	Chapter Eight
• A Meaningful Year in My Past	
• My Golden Nuggets	Chapters Eight, Nine, Ten
• My Story: Capturing a Positive Experience from My Past	Chapter Eight
• My Identity in the Past; . . . in the Present	Chapters Eight, Nine
• A Symbol of Who I Have Been; . . . Am Now;	Chapters Eight,
.Am *Really;* My True Self	Nine, Ten, Eleven
• Holes and Empty Places	Chapters Eight, Nine
• Where Am I?	Chapters Eight, Nine, Ten
• Sit and Reflect	Chapters Eight, Nine, Ten
• My Story: Rescripting a Challenging Experience	Chapter Nine
• My Personal Integration: Where Am I?	Chapter Ten
• My Own Shifts	
• My Own Repeated Encounter	
• Healing Strategies	Chapter Eleven
• My Resources for Becoming	
• What Have You Noticed and Discovered?	
• I Imagine Myself Becoming Someone Who . . .	
• Voice Lessons	

Section Three: Recommended Resources
• Books About Midlife
• Cinema Therapy

Books About Midlife

The following resources focus specifically on the midlife years and, in some cases, beyond that timeframe. No doubt, you are familiar with some of them. Some are excellent for clients to read as "homework" or for independent exploration.

✐**NOTE:** The book's Bibliography is a useful professional resource. It offers the clinician a range and a variety of books and articles in the field of personal transformation.

Arriene, Angeles. *The Second Half of Life: Opening the Eight Gates of Wisdom.* Boulder, Colorado: Sounds True, Inc., 2007.

Bender, Sue. *Everyday Sacred: A Woman's Journey Home.* New York: HarperCollins Publishers, 1995.

Bolen, Jean Shinoda. *Crossing to Avalon: A Woman's Midlife Pilgrimage.* N.Y.: HarperCollins Publishers, 1994.

Borysenko, Joan. *A Woman's Book of Life: The Biology, Psychology, and Spirituality of the Feminine Life Cycle.* New York: Riverhead Books, 1986.

Brewi, Janice, and Anne Brennan. *Mid-Life Spirituality and Jungian Archetypes.* York Beach, ME: Nicolas-Hays, 1988, 1999.

Chinen, Allen B. (1992). *Once Upon a Midlife: Classic Stories and Mythic Tales to Illuminate the Middle Years.* New York: Putnam's Sons, 1992.

Duerk, Judith. *Circle of Stones: A Woman's Journey to Herself.* Philadelphia: Innisfree Press, Inc., 1999.

_____. *I Sit Listening to the Wind: Woman's Encounter Within Herself.* San Diego: LuraMedia, 1993.

Echlin, Kim. *Inanna: From the Myths of Ancient Sumer.* Toronto: Groundwood Books, 2003.

Estes, Clarissa Pinkola. *Women Who Run with the Wolves.* New York: Ballantine, 1992.

Freund, Alexandra M., and Johannes O. Ritter. "Midlife Crisis: A Debate." *Gerontology* 55, no. 5 (2009): 582-91.

Hardin, Paula Payne. *What Are You Doing with the Rest of Your Life?: Choices in Midlife.* San Rafael, CA: New World Library, 1992.

Hollis, James. *Finding Meaning in the Second Half of Life: How to Finally, Really Grow Up.* New York: Gotham Books, 2005.

_____. *The Middle Passage: From Misery to Meaning in Midlife.* Toronto: Inner City Books, 1993.

Jung, Carl. *Memories, Dreams, Reflections,* ed. Aniela Jaffe. New York: Vintage Books, 1965.

_____. *The Red Book* ed. Shamdasani. A publication of the heirs of C.G. Jung and one of the volumes of the Philemon Series. New York: W.W. Norton and Company, 2009.

Kidd, Sue Monk. *The Dance of the Dissident Daughter: A Woman's Journey from Christian Tradition to the Sacred Feminine.* New York: HarperCollins Publishers, Inc., 1996.

_____. *When the Heart Waits.* New York: HarperCollins, 1990.

_____, and Taylor, Anne Kidd. *Travelling with Pomegranates.* New York: Viking, 2009.

Lewinsky, Naomi R. *The Sister From Below: When the Muse Gets Her Way.* New York: Fisher King Press, 2009.

Lewis, Clive S. *Till We Have Faces: A Myth Retold.* New York: Harcourt, Inc., 1956.

Lindbergh, Anne Morrow. *Gift from the Sea.* N.Y.: Pantheon Books, 1955.

McNeely, Deldon Anne. *Becoming: An Introduction to Jung's Concept of Individuation.* Carmel, CA: Fisher King Press, 2010.

Northrup, Christiane. *The Wisdom of Menopause (Revised Edition): Creating Physical and Emotional Health During the Change.* New York: Random House, 2012.
_____. *Women's Bodies, Women's Wisdom: Creating Physical and Emotional Health and Healing.* New York: Random House, 2010.

Palmer, Parker J. *A Hidden Wholeness: The Journey Toward An Undivided Life.* San Francisco: Jossey-Bass, 2004.

Reece, Sachiko Taki. "A Psychological Perspective of Menopause: Sandplay Process As a Rite of Passage." In *Journal of Sandplay Therapy,* 14 no.2 (2005): 115-127.

Rohr, Fr. Richard. *Falling Upward: A Spirituality for the Two Halves of Life.* San Francisco: Jossey-Bass, 2011.

Sheehy, Gail. *The Silent Passage: Revised and Updated Edition.* New York: Random House, 1998

Stein, Murray. *In Mid-life: A Jungian Perspective.* Dallas: Spring Publications, 1983.

Woodman, Marion and Elinor Dickson. *Dancing in the Flames: The Dark Goddess in the Transformation of Consciousness.* Boston: Shambhala Publications, Inc., 1996.
_____. *Leaving My Father's House: A Journey to Conscious Femininity.* Boston: Shambhala Publications, 1992.

_____. *The Pregnant Virgin: A Process of Psychological Transformation.* Toronto, Canada: Inner City Books, 1985.

_____. *Sitting by the Well: Bringing the Feminine to Consciousness Through Language, Dreams, and Metaphor.* (audio) Boulder, Colorado: Sounds True, 1974.

Cinema Therapy

Listed at the end of the book's Bibliography are several films that follow the theme of midlife. Some of these films are recent and others are older. It might be interesting to compare a film's underlying message with your own perspective on midlife and with those of your clients.

Conclusion

No doubt, you have noticed that you can use several of the exercises, tools, and resources for more than one purpose with clients. There is plenty of room for you to bring your unique style, theoretical leanings, and best judgment for a client's welfare to your choice of Midlife Check-In materials and resources.

Depending on where you are in your own life journey—looking back on your middle years, navigating midlife now, or approaching these years—you will bring your unique energy, skills, awareness, and reflection to this work with clients in midlife.

Honor your own journey by being open and curious about your clients' journeys. Expect each of their journeys to be different and, at the same time, to be carrying Nature's agenda for inner transformation—whatever the client's stage of growth and Self awareness may be.

And remember to take time for yourself, and climb up into the support and embrace of your own special tree . . .

APPENDICES

Appendix A:
What's Normal? What's Not?

Appendix B:
Healthy and Unhealthy Responses to Midlife

Appendix C:
Symbols of the Self

> *"One absorbs experiences into the inner stream of consciousness and unconsciousness and, with meditation and focus, wisdom evolves."*
> Peg, Full-Moon Woman, age 81

Appendix A: What's Normal? What's Not?©
MarthaElin Mountain, Ed.D., M.A., MFT

As our values shift and the foundations of our previous assumptions about life begin crumbling during our midlife years, we enter a period of feeling uncertain and anxious. We may feel unsure, even undeserving, of our achievements. Our thinking may feel cloudy; we are not sure if we really know what we know. For women, peri-menopause can bring on a feeling of disorientation and short-term memory loss. These are normal experiences in midlife and important parts of our development.

"Perhaps there is nothing (terribly) wrong. Everyone may feel this way at times. Maybe it will just go away . . . On the other hand, it could get worse . . . I do have some nagging thoughts . . .

'Life has lost its meaning for me.'
'Sometimes I actually consider running away—seriously!'
'I feel like I am becoming a stranger to myself.'
'The very ground under me is moving, throwing me off-balance. It's an earthquake of sorts . . ."

Adjustments in Midlife

Here are the six basic ways in which the adjustments and challenges
of midlife can show up in our lives:

Anxious Mood
Depressed Mood
Physical Symptoms
Decline in Work Ability
Changes in Social Behavior
Mixture of Emotional Symptoms

> Appendix A addresses the first two,
> Anxious Mood and Depressed Mood.

☑ Out Your Symptoms

The charts below highlight the concerns and mood responses we
may experience in our midlife years. They indicate which of these are
usually considered "normal" or "of concern."

How to Use the Charts in Appendix A

Use the charts to explore concerns and mood responses you may
be experiencing in midlife. Follow the directions in three steps:

Step 1. Read a symptom statement.
Example: *"Anxiety comes and goes according to the stresses of my life."*

Step 2. Decide if the statement is true for you or not.

Step 3. If you decide the symptom is true for you, look at the
box, to the right of the symptom. It tells if the symptom is *generally*
considered to be a "normal" experience or if it is *generally* of clinical
concern.

An Example:

Symptom statement:

Anxiety comes and goes according to the stresses of my life. → Normal

⊘ **PLEASE NOTE: These charts are *not* intended for diagnosing!** To make a clinical diagnosis requires professional training and insight. It requires the consideration of a wide range of medical and psychological factors which are not included here. If you are concerned about symptoms you experience, make an appointment with your physician to discuss your concerns and have them evaluated appropriately.

ANXIOUS MOOD
TRIGGERED BY REAL-LIFE EVENTS

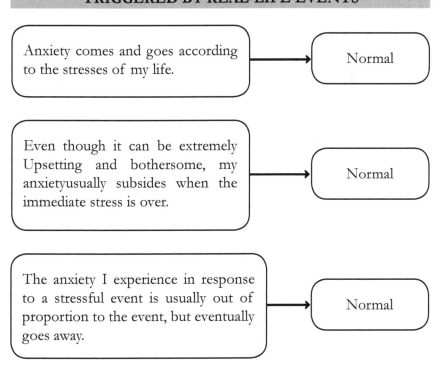

Anxiety comes and goes according to the stresses of my life. → Normal

Even though it can be extremely Upsetting and bothersome, my anxietyusually subsides when the immediate stress is over. → Normal

The anxiety I experience in response to a stressful event is usually out of proportion to the event, but eventually goes away. → Normal

ANXIOUS MOOD
TRIGGERED BY REAL-LIFE EVENTS, Continued:

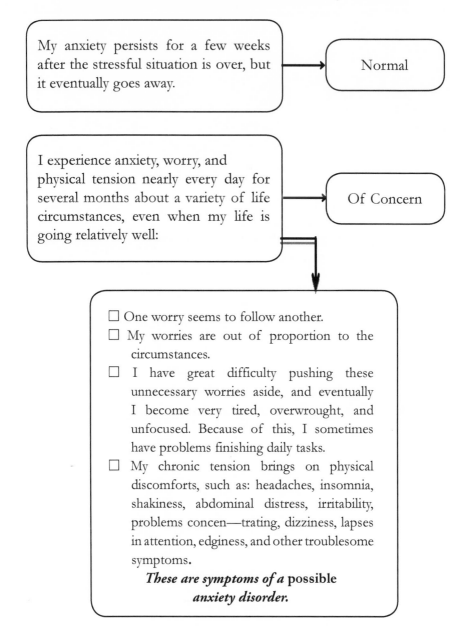

My anxiety persists for a few weeks after the stressful situation is over, but it eventually goes away. → Normal

I experience anxiety, worry, and physical tension nearly every day for several months about a variety of life circumstances, even when my life is going relatively well: → Of Concern

☐ One worry seems to follow another.

☐ My worries are out of proportion to the circumstances.

☐ I have great difficulty pushing these unnecessary worries aside, and eventually I become very tired, overwrought, and unfocused. Because of this, I sometimes have problems finishing daily tasks.

☐ My chronic tension brings on physical discomforts, such as: headaches, insomnia, shakiness, abdominal distress, irritability, problems concen—trating, dizziness, lapses in attention, edginess, and other troublesome symptoms.

These are symptoms of a **possible** *anxiety disorder.*

ANXIOUS MOOD
TRIGGERED BY IMAGE CONCERNS

I imagine a defect in my appearance and feel insecure about it.	→ Normal for nearly everyone
I believe that one of my body parts is deformed, defective, or ugly—in spite of reassurances that it is, in fact, normal. I blow out of proportion any minor imperfections of mine that exist.	→ NOT Normal for nearly everyone
My intense preoccupations about my body are usually focused on facial features, hair, skin imperfections, breasts, genitals, hands, or feet.	→ NOT Normal for nearly everyone
I go to extremes to avoid social contact. I avoid mirrors or I constantly check my imagined or exaggerated defect.	→ NOT Normal for nearly everyone

> ✐**NOTE:** Feeling uncertain and anxious are normal experiences in our midlife years. They are important parts of our development. Having to wrestle with our memories, feelings, and insecurities in this "in-between" place is a healthy and essential part of deepening our self-awareness and meeting new truths of who we are.
>
> In addition to normal anxiety that is triggered by life events, changes, and image concerns, the following symptoms or factors may also be related to one's anxiety in midlife: mild depression, feelings of panic, substance abuse, adjustment to normal life shifts. *If you are experiencing any of these, please consider seeking professional support.*

DEPRESSED MOOD

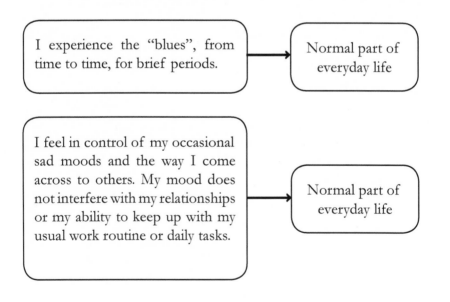

DEPRESSED MOOD, continued:

My moods come and go according to my life circumstances. → Normal part of everyday life

I am able to shift my focus or change my mind-set when sadness comes up for me. → Normal part of everyday life

I am aware of my moods and manage them without feeling trapped by them. → Normal part of everyday life

As a midlifer, I feel a deep sense of loss of what used to be true about me and about my life. It feels as if what was once true isn't anymore; what I knew to be true is changing into someone I do not recognize. → Normal In midlife

DEPRESSED MOOD, continued:

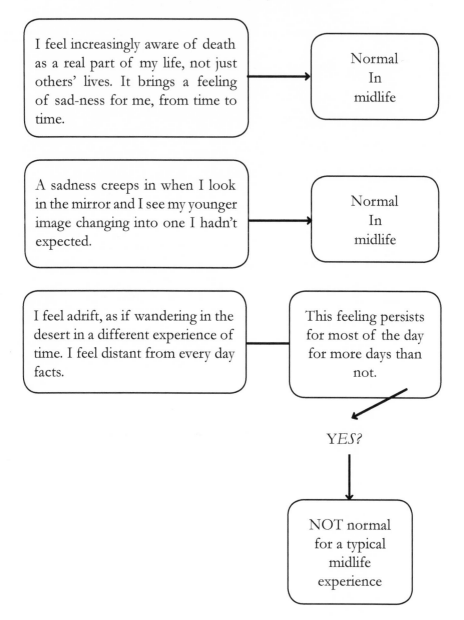

I feel increasingly aware of death as a real part of my life, not just others' lives. It brings a feeling of sad-ness for me, from time to time.

→ Normal In midlife

A sadness creeps in when I look in the mirror and I see my younger image changing into one I hadn't expected.

→ Normal In midlife

I feel adrift, as if wandering in the desert in a different experience of time. I feel distant from every day facts.

This feeling persists for most of the day for more days than not.

YES?

NOT normal for a typical midlife experience

DEPRESSED MOOD, continued:

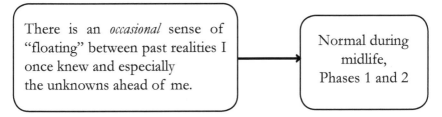

There is an *occasional* sense of "floating" between past realities I once knew and especially the unknowns ahead of me.

→ Normal during midlife, Phases 1 and 2

✍**NOTE:** Several factors interact and influence each other to contribute to a depressed or chronically sad state. These include: biology, body chemistry, genetics, stress, personality patterns, and negative attitudes. Diagnoses for thyroid issues, ADHD, PTSD, and specific situations such as bereavement are not diagnoses of depression.

According to findings from the Study of Women's Health Across the Nation (SWAN), a multiethnic study of women's health at midlife (2007, 2011), a woman's odds for developing depressive symptoms rise as she moves through the menopausal transition. SWAN findings *suggest* that peri-menopause and early post-menopause are a high-risk time for major depression.

"Some women may be particularly vulnerable to the changing hormonal milieu and the unpredictability of menstrual cycles that mark the transition." Given this, however, depression is *not* an *assumed* experience for women in midlife.

Harvard Women's Health Watch, June 2011, p.6

Depression Can Also Come From:

• Not doing meaningful work

• Not knowing what one wants to contribute to this world

• Not willing to be challenged, to leave one's comfort zone

• Not being touched and moved by life's experience

• Not being open to different options and possibilities

• Needing medicines of the heart: humor, joy, laughter, and love

ౘ

- HEALTHY
- PROACTIVE   Talk with a professional
- POSITIVE   Join a support group
- SELF-GROWING   Share concerns and questions with
                       my partner

↑   Talk things over with a trusted
                       friend

                     Reach out and help others, whether
                       they be within my current circle
                       of family and friends or in the
                       larger community

↑   Spend more time with people who
                       have positive attitudes about
                       themselves and others and less
                       time with those who tend to be
                       negative

                     Think about positive people I ad-
                       mire and the ways they have dealt
                       with their own challenges

                     Notice my self-talk, especially self-
                       criticisms and negative beliefs
                       about me and my life

↑   Reconnect with interests I aban-
                       doned at some point and that
                       might have different meaning for
                       me now

257

Update my personal appearance
and style to reflect my shift into

Have a complete physical and
discuss results with physician
in the context of current stage
adulthood; honor favorite colors-
of-life emotional and physical
experiences

- -

Actively seek approval and love
from outside of myself

Blame others when things go
"wrong"

Blame myself for anything that
seems to go awry

Act "as if" I am in my 20s

Buy "toys" and symbols of youth
to recapture my younger self-
image

Have an affair

Numb myself with substance use
or abuse, workaholism, perpetual
busyness, internet pursuits

• UNHEALTHY

• SELF-DESTRUCTIVE   Isolate/disconnect myself from the
mainstreams of my life

• IN DENIAL   Consider ending my life

Appendix C: Symbols of the Self

Various images and forms have been used by individuals and groups, through time and across cultures, to represent the idea of "Self." Scan the lists below, and notice which images and forms you resonate with or which ones "call" to you at this time.

The meaning of "Self" is not inherent in these objects or images. It has been ascribed to them by people who relate the idea of "Self" with the images in a particular context.

Thus, you are the meaning-maker, or the symbol-maker, when you identify an image or object as a representation of "Self." Perhaps there is something that is not included on this list which, *for you*, has a strong association with the concept of "Self?"

℘

Geometrical Structures
Circle
Square
Star
Golden ball or egg
Mandala design

Number
4 and multiples of 4
A 4-fold image

Gemstones
Diamonds
Sapphires
Stones that represent high and rare value

Structures
Castles
Churches
Vessels
Containers
Wheel (with center and spokes radiating outward in a circular rim)

Human Figures That Represent Superiority to the Ego
King
Queen
Princess
Prince
Innocent child

Animal Images
Totem animals that represent one's clan or people
Elephant
Horse
Bull
Bear
Fish
Snake (a paradoxical symbol:

Organic Images
Trees
Flowers
Plants
Lakes
Mountains
Single island in the middle of a lake

Nonorganic Images
Chalice, like the grail
Difficult-to-obtain treasure

Other Images or Objects That Suggest the Meaning of "Self" to
You:

Acceptance
Acknowledgement that something exists or is true; an awareness of how something is and acknowledging it as such; Ex: knowing that suffering is a natural part of life and cannot be avoided; acceptance of self is knowing oneself as unavoidably flawed

Aging
A process of growth by which the mystery of life is slowly revealed to us; "an improvisational art form calling for imagination and willingness to learn" (M.C. Bateson)

Anima
(See "Feminine traits within us.")

Animus
(See "Masculine traits within us.:)

Archetype/archetypal energy
Universal pattern of thought or behavior which is common to humanity; usually recognized as an idea or image; basic content of religions, mythologies, legends, dreams, fantasies, art, and fairy tales. Primary examples include: old, wise person; earth mother; innocent child; shadow; innocent maiden; puer; loneliness; separation; love; compassion. Usually hold a positive and negative energy which acts like a magnet between two poles

Assessment
An appraisal, estimation, or evaluation; an agreed-upon approach to gathering information on which to base decisions or judgments (See also: Self-assessment.)

Assumption
Something one supposes is true or takes for granted without knowing for certain it is true; Ex: magical thinkers assume all good is rewarded and all evil is punished in our world; Ex: assuming that one's inherent value is measured by physical appearance, finances, etc.

Attachment
Objects, people, images, experiences, possessions a person identifies with as a definition of personal identity or value

Authenticity
One's individual true nature or Self; one's original state of unconscious wholeness

Authentic Nature
The inner place and way of being that is balanced, nonjudgmental; called "divine energy" by some; place of one's inner integration

Autobiographical Self
The unique dignity of a human being, derived from our lived past and our anticipated future which are continually built and remodeled, both consciously and unconsciously

Awareness
Consciousness; having knowledge of something

Baby Boomer
The generation of people born between 1956 and 1964. (See Chapter Nine for a detailed list of what is associated with this generation.)

Becoming
Changing or developing; growing into a way of being; growing to be in a certain state; (Philosophy) Any change from the lower level of potentiality to the higher level of actuality; undergoing

Body Messages
Sensations your body creates in response to emotions that your brain is processing; Ex: tightness in chest, headaches, nausea, choked-up feeling in throat, increased pulse

Boundaries
Clear lines between what is you and what is not you, between what is your responsibility and what is not, between what you will tolerate and what you will not, and between what you control and what you do not control (Enns and Black: "It's Not Ok Anymore.")

Calling
An ideal or vision that moves you from a deep place inside and will not go away, even if you postpone or avoid it

Catharsis
A clearing or resolution of a suppressed emotion through intellectual recognition, confirmation by the heart, and actual release of the emotion

Choice Point
A critical moment or potential turning point when one must make a decision or a choice about what will happen next; the point of opportunity for making a difference

Consciousness
The part of the mind of which we are aware and about which we can verbalize

Containers
Objects or various structures, plans or timeframes designed to keep feelings, actions, information from getting out of control; places one can imagine or create to put concerns, feelings, dreams in temporarily

Courage
Originally "coeur," French for heart; willingness to let go of who you think you should be in order to be who you are

Defenses
Self-protective behaviors that can sometimes interfere, at times, consciously or unconsciously, with one's healthy personal freedom and, at other times, can enable one's ego to defend against unbearable trauma in order to survive; Self-protective behaviors that may be conscious or unconscious

Dream
Symbolic expression of the unconscious; a vivid, uncensored representation of one's ideals and desires, challenges, fears, and hidden desires; reveals aspects of oneself that are not normally conscious; Brain circuits that govern emotions, sensations, and memories (vs. rational thought and reality) are active during dreaming.

Ego
A little ship on the huge ocean of who you are *really*; day-to-day awareness; the smaller part of yourself that assumes it knows all and is running the show; many habits and patterns developed to keep one safe; can become a barrier against true communication and communion with the deeper places in oneself; roughly equivalent to consciousness; A healthy ego gives us permission to explore things that are beyond rational knowing.

Emotional Needs
Four basic human needs for healthy development: feeling loved, feeling we belong, feeling safe, feeling worthy.

Empty Places
Unmet emotional needs in us; inner emotional voids; can be created by loss, rejection, longing, unfulfilled dreams; childhood emotional wounding; painful feelings and negative beliefs we acquired early in life; revealed to us through feelings such as deep disappointment, low self-worth, long-held anger,

hopelessness, longing to be seen or heard, fear of telling one's truth or using one's true voice (MarthaElin Mountain)

False Self
One's adapted, passive, conforming self; the part that alters behaviors, represses true feelings, and pushes one's needs aside to fit in with others; motivated by desire to survive

Feminine Traits Within Us (the "Anima")
"Anima" from the feminine form of the Latin word for "soul," the complement of "animus;" Associated traits: nurturing, patient, calm, empathic, heartful, compassionate aspects; celebrating diversity, individuality, capacity for art and creativity; service to others, protecting; moods; receptive to the non-rational; oneness with nature. Wisdom and intuition (secret knowing) are also associated with the feminine. Psychologically healthy individuals have a balance of feminine and masculine traits and express them in positive ways. (See "Masculine Traits Within Us [the "Animus"]).

Full-Moon Phase
Psychological phase of life following the three phases of midlife; timing depends on choices and decisions made during midlife; core question: "What is the meaning of my life?"; (MarthaElin Mountain)

Generation X-er
The generation of people born between 1965 and 1981; (See Chapter Nine for a detailed list of what is associated with this generation.)

Gnosis
Inner knowing: the certainty a person feels when she responds from a deep recognition (or "knowing") of something within her; an inner certainty of courage to trust a choice he is making as an authentic and meaningful one; an intuitive knowing of something invisible to us

Golden Boomer
Generation of people born between 1946 and 1955; (See Chapter Nine for a detailed list of what is associated with this generation.)

Golden Nuggets
Personal resources, such as acquired skills, lessons learned, experiences of pain and suffering, knowledge and expertise, courage to act, compassion, insights, healthy boundaries, triumphs, relationship experiences; personal assets to be "mined" in times of decision making, unexpected change, various life challenges. (MarthaElin Mountain)

Healing (vs. Curing)
Resolving, repairing, or mending emotional wounds; restoring one's emotional or spiritual wholeness

Heroic Thinking
Thinking approach of older adolescents and young adults who seek to conquer the dangers and challenges in life and to gain recognition for doing so

Human Thinking
Thinking approach of mature human beings who use reason and logic and consider earlier life lessons when making choices or decisions; includes compassion and concern for others' welfare, acceptance of life's many facets, including suffering, love, and responsibility

Identity
A person's sense of who she is, based upon what she assumes is true about the world and her place in it, about other people, and about what gives her value; the personal myth or story one constructs to define who he is; We modify, adjust, and transform our identities throughout our lifetime.

Individuation
Lifelong process of becoming one's true Self; "The process of maturation and realizing that which we are inherently capable of becoming" (Goethe); involves an increasing awareness of one's ego, including strengths and limitations; goal is to divest one's self of the false wrappings of the persona; an internal subjective process of integration

Inner Child
The aspect of you who is naturally spontaneous and creative, who loves to play and to feel joy, is curious and wonders; the part whose inherent and delightful energy is still available to you, when you connect with and nurture it *(See also:* Wounded Child)

Inner Knowing
(See "Gnosis.")

Integration
One's inner process of growing into true Self, Nature's intended inner wholeness; the gradual process of overlapping between conscious and hidden aspects of our self

Intimacy
A quality of familiar, affectionate, personal terms; suggests very close ties that move oneself to become vulnerable; qualities of closeness in relationships and other personal pursuits that matter deeply

Intuition
A secret "knowing;" a faculty of our higher potential that picks up what is in a person's inner world: "Content presents itself whole and complete without our being able to explain or discover how this content came into existence." (Carl Jung); psychic function that perceives possibilities inherent in the present; does not depend on logic

Magical Thinking

Thinking approach of a young child: believing that things are true because one wishes them to be, that goodness is always rewarded and wickedness always punished in this world; young people and adults may choose life partners based on the belief that a "magical other" will rescue and take care of them

Mandala

A Sanskrit word that means center, circumference, or magic circle. A circular design that mirrors the Self in that moment. Drawing, painting, and dreaming mandalas is a natural part of the individuation process. Mandalas range from very simple to very complex.

Manipulation

Shrewd or devious management of people, circumstances, or things, especially for one's own advantage

Masculine Traits Within Us (the "Animus")

"Animus" from the masculine form of the Latin word for "soul;" Associated traits: planning and goal setting; productive, go-getting achievement orientation; logical thinking; independence; celebrating competition, power over others; drive to win, stubbornness, coldness, courage, domineering, critical judgment, using words like "always," "should," "must." Psychologically healthy individuals have a balance of masculine and feminine traits and express them in positive ways. (See: "Feminine Traits Within Us [the "Anima"])

Mask (See also "Persona.")

Different energies that ebb and flow through us throughout our lives and take form as masks, or personas, we wear to help us navigate life; Dionysus is considered god of the mask.

Meaning

The experience of having a sense of purpose that grows from inside of us to the outside

Menopausal Transition
The period of time in which a woman experiences peri-menopause, menopause, and post-menopause; includes physical, psychological, social, and spiritual aspects; gateway to "second adulthood"; ends the traditional meaning of "femininity" as menstruation, fertility, childbearing; "It is all about getting your brain to adjust to a lower level of estrogen." (Roberta Diaz Brinton, USC Neuropharmacologist)

Midlife
A primarily psychological shift, occurring typically during one's early 40s through mid—or late 60s, that pushes us to move away from the "false" selves (or personas) of earlier years toward our true Self or wholeness; period when the psyche begins to undergo a transformation, urging the person to turn inward and examine the meaning of her life and to focus on her inner self

Midlife Crisis
A popular concept (and myth) describing middle adulthood; a misguided assumption is that a crisis is *necessary and expected* in midlife; being at the midpoint of life and feeling incomplete, as if something crucial is missing; a period of midlife reassessment and revision of one's life story; a period of significant changes in self-understanding with strong implications for the meaning of one's life; turning inward to examine the meaning of one's life

Midlife (Core) Skills
Being self-aware, managing one's self in healthy ways, accepting what is that one cannot change

Mood
A temporary emotional state, such as a sad, joyful, anxious mood, that can be brought on by perceptions and beliefs (what you tell yourself), or by chemical imbalances

Mortality
The fact of death and dying; natural element of being alive

Not-knowing
The place in us without *concrete* answers; the place that knows more than we do and that is more than we are

Persona (See also "Mask.")
The image of ideal and protective aspects one presents to the outer world; different roles of the true Self. a public personality that helps us navigate the world; A persona may hide our true feelings or thoughts. Whether or not we are conscious of the mask we wear is important to its being more positive or negative in nature. When we play with a mask, know we wear one, and are conscious of playing a role, the persona is more positive. When unconscious of wearing a mask, we tend to over identity with it as being our true Self and, thus, it becomes more negative. When one's personality is balanced the persona will be developed, but not to the exclusion of other parts of oneself.

Perspective
Mental view or outlook; a way of looking at or thinking about something

Psyche
The totality of all our psychological processes, both conscious and unconscious; "a boiling cauldron of contradictory impulses, inhibitions, and affects" (Carl G. Jung); a complicated interplay of many factors, such as a person's age, sex, hereditary disposition, psychological type and attitude, and degree of conscious control over the instincts; continually active within our being, sometimes at a more conscious level than at other times

Regression
Looking back for something that used to be; sometimes prompted by one's inability to adapt to changing circumstances; a necessary part in our psychological development and progress

Repression
A deliberate intention of the conscious mind to avoid recollecting a memory because it would be painful or disagreeable; Ego generally represses material that would disturb peace of mind.

Second Adulthood
Approximately the late 30s through the later years of life

Self
Our unconscious striving for centeredness, wholeness, and meaning; the archetype of wholeness; helps us make choices that are true to our most authentic nature; the entire person of an individual; your deepest being and truest nature; the center of your being; connection with the Self like having one's own North Star drawn to a deeper wisdom; ultimately, a mystery within us that is larger than we will ever understand fully; When you are true to your Self, you defend your integrity, the totality of the psyche, which includes the ego. Self appears in dreams, myths, and fairytales. (See also: "False Self," "True Self," and "Tree.")

Self-assessment
An evaluation or judgment of one's own experience, abilities

Self-Awareness
The capacity for introspection and self-reflection; what catches a person's attention about her—or himself; an inner-knowing of one's self

Self-concept
The image, the picture, and the set of perceptions and feelings which one has of one's self and one's characteristic behavior patterns; results from interpersonal relationships; images and accompanying stories we have about our self created by our imagination

Self-Management
Ability to take care of oneself and make healthy choices for one's life; ability to *choose* behaviors, thoughts, and feelings (vs. acting, thinking, and feeling automatically, as by habit)

Self-worth
Sense of one's own value or worth as a person; the quality of being worthy of esteem

Shadow
Those traits and feelings that we cannot admit to ourselves; opposite of our persona; an archetypal energy; hidden or unconscious aspects of oneself, both positive and negative; undeveloped, unexpressed potentials of all kinds; all those things about oneself or one's culture with which one is uncomfortable or that one is not proud of; that which has not entered adequately into consciousness; those personal characteristics that the ego or conscious personality forgets, neglects, or buries because it does not want to acknowledge them, only to discover them in uncomfortable confrontations with others. Inner development can emerge only when we risk a confrontation with the neglected parts of ourselves.

Shifts
Inner changes of direction or psychological conditions, driven from within us, occurring across our life phases and experiences of the maturation process

Sorting
An inner process of turning over inside of us the possibilities and choices to see which one or ones *feel right*; getting an inner sense of how one feels about something (MarthaElin Mountain)

Soul
"The light hidden inside the dark that secretly holds things together within each of us and with the world" (Margaret Meade); "something deeper and wiser within us; timeless part of our self" (Jean Shinoda Bolen)

Suffering
A part of life experienced through pain of loneliness, failure, separation, and loss; a pulling of our soul into the depths of dark places, due to the natural ebb and flow of our psychic energy; an inevitable part of the human experience that no amount of denial or "good work" can prevent; Mythical stories of separation and loss often heal suffering via human sharing and compassion. To move through and beyond suffering one must let go of the desire to control (Buddha).

Symbol
An image or object that represents something else by association or resemblance; a material object used to represent something invisible; something we assign meaning to to hold that meaning, in a nonverbal form, for something else; something which expresses what is essentially unknown, unexplained, or which eludes our present knowledge; a container that can hold meaning for us while we are integrating a deeper experience

Symptom
A condition in our body or behavior that suggests an imbalance of some kind—physical, emotional, spiritual, mental; may hold information about what is needed and, in this way, may be a type of symbol for the dis-ease or imbalance

Tasks
Core developmental challenges typical for each stage of maturation and growth from birth to our last years. One must complete the psychological tasks of one developmental stage in order to accomplish those of the next developmental stage. Ex: An adult task is to accept that muck and mire states of life are transitory, unavoidable, and require suffering.

Threads of Becoming
The seven facets of our human experience that weave the fabric of who and how we become as we mature in life: authenticity, body, creative energy, heart, identity, loss and grief, relationship (MarthaElin Mountain); See Chapter Six.

Threshold

A beginning; a physical or psychological "plank" to step over into a new place; the point at which one perceives increasing strength or produces a new response in life

Trait

A factor in one's temperament which one is born with; some traits are genetically transmitted; some are strongly influenced by early developmental factors such as environment; Ex: level of sensitivity, intensity, persistence, adaptability (See also: "Masculine traits within us," "Feminine traits within us.")

Tree (as symbol)

In alchemy: the nature of intense inner life and development; reveals the "evergreen" within the individual. a link between the heavens and the underworld, signifying regeneration; associated with eternity; a living process of enlightenment; growth from below upwards and growth from above downwards; symbol of hope, vitality, and transformation; one's deep meaning and purpose that grow from the inside out; maternal qualities, protective shelter; cycle of death and rebirth in nature; Shamans and seers traditionally used trees as bridges to the realms of the spirits.

True Self

The core of who one is—*really*—that gives one a sense of being alive, real, and creative; nonjudgmental self; includes many masks and roles (See also: "Mask," "Persona," "Self.")

Turning Point

Growth points as seen in retrospect: An event that symbolizes a significant change in one's life; an experience of undergoing a significant change in one's understanding of self

Unconscious

The part of the mind that is not accessible to us and which houses some of the most intense urges, feelings, and desires that drive us; the majority of our mind; It will move us whether we like it or not. It speaks to us primarily through dreams.

Visualization
A process of using one's natural power of imagination to create an idea, picture, or blueprint in one's mind

Vulnerability
Willingness to do something where there are no guarantees; willingness to let yourself be seen; willingness to lean into your story and pain

Wholeheartedness
Living from a deep personal sense of worthiness

Wholeness
A more naturally balanced relationship between the ego and the Self which gives one the opportunity to live life in a more conscious, authentic manner

Wisdom
Insight into human nature; a developmental task that requires us to confront ourselves and to reflect on our experiences; an enlargement of our vision of what is possible; arises through our own assimilated experiences of suffering; required for dealing effectively with interpersonal problems; practical understanding; increases trust in the intuition of our heart; "Wisdom is the art of knowing what to overlook." (William James, 1890)

Wonder
A state one is in when living with apparently insoluble questions; an invitation to useful hints and clues to emerge in one for increased understanding of something

Worthiness
A strong sense of love and belonging

Wounded Inner Child

The part of us that experienced primal wounding through physical or emotional abandonment or overwhelm in our childhood; the part living with a distorted sense of self due to its early wounding; something in us that is shut down; a search for feeling loved; pleasing others and neglecting personal needs); Early wounding is played out unconsciously in adult choices and relationships (ex: a power drive for recognition and respect.)

ଓ

Bibliography

The Bibliography includes a wide variety of resources: books, articles, and films. You will find among them valuable information to support and enhance your exploration and understanding of the psychology, science, and mythology underlying the midlife years. Some of my personal favorites are among these resources; I encourage you to find yours. The separate listing, "Films Focused on Midlife," is included at the end of the Bibliography.

American Psychiatric Association. *Diagnostic Manual and Statistical Manual of Mental Disorders, DSM-IV-TR Fourth Edition, Text Revision*. Washington, D.C.: American Psychiatric Association, 2000.

Arriene, Angeles. *The Second Half of Life: Opening the Eight Gates of Wisdom*. Boulder, Colorado: Sounds True, Inc., 2007.

Artress, Lauren. *Walking a Sacred Path: Rediscovering the Labyrinth As a Spiritual Tool*. N.Y.: The Berkley Publishing Group, 1995.

Baltes, Margaret, and Laura L. Carstensen. "The Process of Successful Aging: Selection, Optimization, and Compensation." In *Understanding Human Development: Dialogues with Lifespan Psychology*. Edited by U. Staudinger, Chapter Five. Netherlands: Kluwer Academic Publisher Group, 2003.

Barks, C., Trans. *The Essential Rumi*. Edison, N.J.: Castle Books, 1997.

Bateson, Mary Catherine. *Composing a Life*. New York: Grove Press, 2001.

_____. *Composing a Further Life: The Age of Active Wisdom*. New York: Knopf, 2010.

Bender, Sue. *Everyday Sacred: A Woman's Journey Home*. New York: HarperCollins Publishers, 1995.

Bolen, Jean Shinoda. *Crossing to Avalon: A Woman's Midlife Pilgrimage*. N.Y.: HarperCollins Publishers, 1994.

_____. *Goddesses in Every Woman: Powerful Archetypes in Women's Lives*. New York: Harper Collins, 1984, 2004.

_____. *Like a Tree: How Trees, Women, and Tree People Can Save the Planet*. San Francisco: Conari Press, 2011.

Borysenko, Joan. *A Woman's Book of Life: The Biology, Psychology, and Spirituality of the Feminine Life Cycle*. New York: Riverhead Books, 1986.

_____. *A Woman's Spiritual Retreat: Teaching, Meditations, and Rituals to Celebrate Your Authentic Feminine Wisdom*. (audio) Boulder, Colorado: Sounds True, Inc., 2004.

Bradshaw, John. *Homecoming: Reclaiming and Championing Your Inner Child*. New York: Bantam Books, 1990.

Bradway, Kay. *Villa of Mysteries: Pompeii Initiation Rites of Women*. San Francisco: The C.G. Jung Institute, 1982.

Brewi, Janice, and Anne Brennan. *Mid-Life Spirituality and Jungian Archetypes*. York Beach, ME: Nicolas-Hays, 1988, 1999.

Bridges, William. *Transitions*. New York: Addison-Wesley Publishing Co., 1980.

Brown, Byron. *Soul Without Shame*. Boston: Shambhala Publications, Inc., 1999.

Chaiklin, Sharon, and Hilda Wengrower. *The Art and Science of Dance Movement Therapy: Life Is a Dance*. New York: Routledge, 2009.

Chinen, Allen B. (1992). *Once Upon a Midlife: Classic Stories and Mythic Tales to Illuminate the Middle Years*. New York: Putnam's Sons, 1992.

Chodorow, Joan. *Dance Therapy and Depth Psychology: The Moving Imagination*. New York: Routledge, 1991.

Cirlot, Juan E. *A Dictionary of Symbols*. New York: Philosophical Library, 1993.

Cohen, Gene D. *The Mature Mind: The Positive Power of the Aging Brain*. N.Y.: Basic Books, 2005.

Conway, Deanna J. *Maiden, Mother, Crone*. St. Paul, MN: Llewellyn Publications, 1994.

Cooper, J.C. *Dictionary of Symbols*. London: Thames and Hudson, 1978.

Damasio, Antonio. *The Feeling of What Happens: Body and Emotion in the Making of Consciousness*. Orlando: Harcourt, 1999.

Dass, Ram. *Still Here: Embracing Aging, Changing and Dying*, eds. Mark Matousek and Marlene Roeder. New York: Riverhead Books, 2000.

Dewey, John. *Art As Experience*. New York: Putnam Publishing, 1934.

Doidge, Norman. *The Brain That Changes Itself: Stories of Personal Triumph from the Frontiers of Brain Science.* New York: Penguin Books, 2007.

Duerk, Judith. *Circle of Stones: A Woman's Journey to Herself.* Philadelphia: Innisfree Press, Inc., 1999.

_____. *I Sit Listening to the Wind: Woman's Encounter Within Herself.* San Diego: LuraMedia, 1993.

Eastwood, Pratibha S. *Nine Windows to Wholeness: Exploring Numbers in Sandplay Therapy.* Honolulu: Sanity Press, 2002.

Echlin, Kim. *Inanna: From the Myths of Ancient Sumer.* Toronto: Groundwood Books, 2003.

Edinger, Edward. *Ego and Archetype.* Boston: Shambhala, 1992.

Eliot, Thomas S. *Complete Poems and Plays.* New York: Harcourt, Brace, and World, 1962.

Ensler, Eve. *The Good Body.* New York: Random House, 2004.

Ephron, Nora. *I Feel Bad About My Neck and Other Thoughts on Being a Woman.* New York: A. Knopf, Random House, Inc., 2006.

Erb, Everett, and Douglas Hooker. *The Psychology of the Emerging Self.* Philadephia: F.A. Davis Co., 1971.

Estes, Clarissa Pinkola *The Creative Fire: Myths and Stories on the Cycles of Creativity.* (audio) Boulder, Colorado: Sounds True, 1991.

_____. *Women Who Run with the Wolves.* New York: Ballantine, 1992.

Feinstein, David and Stanley Krippner. *Personal Mythology: The Psychology of Your Evolving Self. Using Ritual, Dreams, and Imagination to Discover Your Inner Story*. Los Angeles: Jeremy P. Tarcher, Inc., 1998.

Fincher, Susanne F. *Creating Mandalas for Insight, Healing, and Self-Expression*. Boston: Shambbala Publications, Inc, 1991.

Fosha, Diana, and Daniel Siegel, Marion Solomon, eds. *The Healing Power of Emotion: Affective Neuroscience, Development, and Clinical Practice*. New York: W.W. Norton and Co., 2009.

Freund, Alexandra M., and Johannes O. Ritter. "Midlife Crisis: A Debate." *Gerontology* 55, no. 5 (2009): 582-91.

Gardner, Howard. *Extraordinary Minds: Portraits of 4 Exceptional Individuals and an Examination of Our Own Extraordinariness*. New York: BasicBooks, HarperCollins Publishers, Inc., 1997.

Green, Liz, and Juliet Sharman-Burke. *The Mythic Journey: The Meaning of Myth As A Guide for Life*. New York: Simon and Schuster, 2000.

Greene, Maxine. *Releasing the Imagination: Essays on Education, the Arts, and Social Change*. San Francisco: Jossey-Bass, Inc., 1995.

Hancock, Emily. *The Girl Within*. New York: Fawcett Columbine, 1989.

Hardin, Paula Payne. *What Are You Doing with the Rest of Your Life?: Choices in Midlife*. San Rafael, CA: New World Library, 1992.

Henderson, Joseph L. "Images of Initiation." In *Journal of Sandplay Therapy*, 3 no.1 (1993): 45-55.

Henderson, Joseph L. *Shadow and Self: Selected Papers in Analytical Psychology*. New York: Chiron Pub., 1990.

Hillman, James. *The Force of Character and the Lasting Life*. New York: Random House Publishing, 1999.

Hollis, James. *Finding Meaning in the Second Half of Life: How to Finally, Really Grow Up.* New York: Gotham Books, 2005.

_____. *The Middle Passage: From Misery to Meaning in Midlife.* Toronto: Inner City Books, 1993.

_____. *The Swamplands of the Soul.* New York: Gotham Books, 1998.

Jones, Alan. *Soul Making.* San Francisco: Harper and Row, 1985.

Johnson, Robert. *He: Understanding Male Psychology.* New York: Harper and Row, 1977.

_____. *Inner Gold.* Kihei, Hawaii: Koa Books, 2008.

_____. *Owning Your Own Shadow: Understanding the Dark Side of the Psyche.* San Francisco: HarperCollins, 1991.

_____. *She: Understanding Feminine Psychology.* New York: Harper and Row, 1977.

Jung, Carl. *Memories, Dreams, Reflections,* ed. Aniela Jaffe. New York: Vintage Books, 1965.

_____. *The Red Book* ed. Shamdasani. A publication of the heirs of C.G. Jung and one of the volumes of the Philemon Series. New York: W.W. Norton and Company, 2009.

_____. "Stages of Life." *The Structure and Dynamics of the Psyche, vol. 8 of Collected Works of C.G. Jung,* Translated by R.F.C. Hull. Princeton: Princeton University Press, 1960, para. 783, 1960.

_____. *Symbols of Transformation. Collected Works (5).* Princeton: Princeton University Press, 1960.

Jung Platform. Meade, M. "The Light Inside Dark Times: Tales of Healing and Change." Accessed March 12, 2012. October 18, 2011. www.jungplatform.com/ondemand-lectures/.

Kaplan, Jill. "Circumambulation: Pointing to the Center in Sandplay Therapy." in *Journal of Sandplay Therapy*, 21 No. 1, (2012): 125-138 . . .

Keirsey, David. *Please Understand Me II: Temperament, Intelligence.* Del Mar, CA.: Prometheus Nemesis Book Company, 1998.

Kidd, Sue Monk. *The Dance of the Dissident Daughter: A Woman's Journey from Christian Tradition to the Sacred Feminine.* New York: HarperCollins Publishers, Inc., 1996.

_____. *When the Heart Waits.* New York: HarperCollins, 1990.

_____, and Taylor, Anne Kidd. *Travelling with Pomegranates.* New York: Viking, 2009.

Kleinman, S. Body Talk: Giving Form to Feelings. Paper presented at the 38th Annual Conference of the American Dance Therapy Association Columbia, Maryland: 2003.

Lewinsky, Naomi R. *The Sister From Below: When the Muse Gets Her Way.* New York: Fisher King Press, 2009

Lewis, Clive S. *Till We Have Faces: A Myth Retold.* New York: Harcourt, Inc., 1956.

Lindbergh, Anne Morrow. *Gift from the Sea.* N.Y.: Pantheon Books, 1955.

McNeely, Deldon Anne. *Becoming: An Introduction to Jung's Concept of Individuation.* Carmel, CA: Fisher King Press, 2010.

Masterson, James F. *The Search for the Real Self: Unmasking the Personality Disorders of Our Age.* New York: The Free Press, 1988.

Mayo Clinic. "Male Menopause: Myth or Reality." Accessed June 17, 2012. July 23, 2011.http://www.mayoclinic.com/health/male-menopause/MC00058.

Miller, Alice. *The Drama of the Gifted Child: The Search for the True Self.* New York: Basic Books, Revised and Updated 2007.

Moacanin, Radmila. *Jung's Psychology and Tibetan Buddhism: Western and Eastern Paths to the Heart.* London: Wisdom Publications, 1986.

Moore, Thomas. *Care of the Soul: A Guide for Cultivating Depth and Sacredness in Everyday Life.* New York: HarperCollins, 1992.

Morena, Gita. "Language of Imagery: Language of Connection." *Journal of Sandplay Therapy,* 14 no.2 (2005): 67-77.

Nelson, Barbara. "Rediscovery of the Golden Child in Sandplay." *Journal of Sandplay Therapy,* 6 no.1 (1997): 123-130.

Northrup, Christiane. *The Wisdom of Menopause (Revised Edition): Creating Physical and Emotional Health During the Change.* New York: Random House, 2012.

_____. *Women's Bodies, Women's Wisdom: Creating Physical and Emotional Health and Healing.* New York: Random House, 2010.

O'Donohue, John. *Anam Cara: A Book of Celtic Wisdom.* New York: HarperCollins, 1997.

Palmer, Parker J. *A Hidden Wholeness: The Journey Toward An Undivided Life.* San Francisco: Jossey-Bass, 2004.

Perlman, M. *The Power of Trees: The Reforesting of the Soul.* Dallas: Spring Publications, 1994.

Reece, Sachiko Taki. "A Psychological Perspective of Menopause: Sandplay Process As a Rite of Passage." In *Journal of Sandplay Therapy,* 14 no.2 (2005): 115-127.

Remen, Rachel Naomi. *Kitchen Table Wisdom: Stories That Heal.* N.Y.: Berkley Publishing Group, 1996.

Rogers-Mitchell, Rie (1994). "Moving Toward Initiation." *Journal of Sandplay Therapy,* 3 no. 2 (1994): 37-57.

Rohr, Fr. Richard. *Falling Upward: A Spirituality for the Two Halves of Life.* San Francisco: Jossey-Bass, 2011.

Rothschild, Babette. *The Body Remembers: The Psychophysiology of Trauma and Trauma Treatment.* New York: W.W. Norton and Co., 2000.

Sheehy, Gail. *Passages: Predictable Crises of Adult Life.* New York: Bantam, 1977.

_____. *The Silent Passage: Revised and Updated Edition.* New York: Random House, 1998.

Siegel, Daniel J. *The Developing Mind: How Relationships and the Brain Interact to Shape Who We Are.* New York: The Guilford Press, 1999.

Singer, Jerome L. "Researching Imaginative Play and Adult Consciousness: Implications for Daily and Literary Creativity." In *Psychology of Aesthetics, Creativity, and the Arts,* 3 no.4 (2009): 190-199. Washington, D.C.: American Psychological Association.

Stein, Murray. *In Mid-life: A Jungian Perspective.* Dallas: Spring Publications, 1983.

_____. *Jung's Map of the Soul: An Introduction.* Peru, Illinois: Open Court Publishing Co., 1998.

Stevens, Wallace. *Collected Poems.* New York: A. Knopf, Inc., 1936.

Storr, Anthony *Solitude: A Return to the Self.* New York: Ballantine Books, 1988.

Strauch, Barbara. *The Secret Life of the Grownup Brain: The Surprsing Talents of the Middle-Aged Mind.* New York: Viking Penguin, 2010.

Ronnberg, Ami and Kathleen Martin, eds. *The Book of Symbols.* Cologne, Germany: 2000.

Viorst, Judith. *Necessary Losses: The Loves, Illusions, Dependencies, and Impossible Expectations That All of Us Have to Give Up in Order to Grow.* New York: Fireside, 1998.

von Franz, Marie-Louise. "The Process of Individuation." In *Man and His Symbols* Edited by Carl G. Jung. Part Three. Garden City, N.Y: Doubleday and Company, 1964.

Vries, Arthur De. *Dictionary of Symbols and Imagery.* Amsterdam: North Holland Publishing, 1984.

Walker, Barbara. *The Woman's Dictionary of Symbols and Sacred Objects.* San Francisco: Harper, 1983.

Whitfield, Charles L. *Boundaries and Relationships: Knowing, Protecting, and Enjoying the Self.* Florida: Health Communications, Inc., 2010.

_____. *A Gift to Myself: A Personal Workbook and Guide to the Bestselling "Healing the Child Within."* Florida: Health Communications, Inc., 1990.

_____. *Healing the Child Within: Discovery and Recovery for Adult Children of Dysfunctional Families.* Florida: Health Communications, Inc., 1987.

Willis, Sherry L., and James D. Reid. *Life in the Middle: Psychological and Social Development in Middle Age.* Sand Diego: Academic Press, 1999.

Winnicott, Donald W. "Ego Distortion in Terms of True and False Self." In *The Maturational Process and the Facilitating Environment: Studies in the Theory of Emotional Development*. 140-152. New York: International UP Inc., 1965.

——————————. *Playing and Reality*. London: Routledge, 1971.

Wood, Nancy. *Spirit Walker: Poems by Nancy Wood, Paintings by Frank Howell*. N.Y.: Delacorte Press, 1993.

Woodman, Marion and Elinor Dickson. *Dancing in the Flames: The Dark Goddess in the Transformation of Consciousness*. Boston: Shambhala Publications, Inc., 1996.

——————————. *Leaving My Father's House: A Journey to Conscious Femininity*. Boston: Shambhala Publications, 1992.

——————————. *The Pregnant Virgin: A Process of Psychological Transformation*. Toronto, Canada: Inner City Books, 1985.

——————————. *Sitting by the Well: Bringing the Feminine to Consciousness Through Language, Dreams, and Metaphor*. (audio) Boulder, Colorado: Sounds True, 1974.

Woolf, Virginia. *A Room of One's Own*. New York: Harcourt, Inc., 1929.

——————————. *Moments of Being*. New York: Harcourt Brace and Co., 1976.

Zukav, Gary. *The Seat of the Soul*. New York: Simon and Schuster, 1989.

Zweig, Connie and Jeremiah Abrams, eds. *Meeting the Shadow: The Hidden Power of the Dark Side of Human Nature*. New York: St. Martin's Press, 1991.

Films Focused on Midlife

American Beauty. DVD. Directed by Sam Mendes. 1999; Glendale, CA: DreamWorks, 1999.

Being Julia. DVD. Directed by Istvan Szabo. 2004; New York City, NY: Sony Pictures Classics, 2004.

Bread and Tulips (Pane e Tulipani). DVD. Directed by Silvio Soldini. 2001. Italy: Amka Films Productions, 2001.

The Bridges of Madison County. Video. Directed by Clint Eastwood. 1995; Los Angeles, CA: Warner Bros., 1995.

Death of a Salesman. Video. Directed by Laszio Benedek. 1951; Hollywood, CA: Columbia Pictures, 1951.

Death of a Salesman. Video. Directed by Voiker Schlondorff. 1985; Germany: CBS made-for-television film, 1985.

Defending Your Life. Video. Directed by Albert Brooks. 1991; Los Angeles, CA: Geffen Pictures, 1991.

Enchanted April. DVD. Directed by Michael Cormac Newell. 1992; United Kingdom: BBC Films, 1992.

Same Time, Next Year. Video. Directed by Robert Mulligan. 1978; Los Angeles, CA: Universal films, 1978.

Everybody's Fine. DVD. Directed by Kirk Jones. 2009; New York City, NY: Miramax Films, 2009.

The Four Seasons. Video. Directed by Alan Alda. 1981; Los Angeles, CA: Universal City Studios, Inc., 1981.

Hannah and Her Sisters. Video. Directed by Woody Allen. 1986; Los Angeles, CA: Orion Pictures Corporation, 1986.

The Hours. DVD. Directed by Stephen Daldry. 2003; Hollywood, CA.: Paramount Pictures, 2003.

It's Complicated. DVD. Directed by Nancy Meyers. 2009; Los Angeles, CA: Universal Studios, 2009.

Kramer vs. Kramer. Video. Directed by Robert Benton. 1979; Hollywood, CA: Columbia Pictures, 1979.

The Misfits. Video. Directed by John Huston. 1961; Los Angeles, CA: Seven Arts Productions, 1961.

Something's Gotta Give. DVD. Directed by Nancy Meyers. 2003. Hollywood, CA: Colombia Pictures Industries, Inc., 2003.

Sullivan's Travels. Video. Directed by Preston Sturges. 1941; Hollywood. CA: Paramount Pictures, 1941.

Index

Q

BACK POCKET
Reflections, Insights, Questions, Observations

My Midlife Checklist© Results

Midlife phase(s) I Am In   ☐ Phase 1 ☐ Phase 2 ☐ Phase 3

My Threads of Becoming

<u>How They Are Weaving into My Life:</u>

☐ **A**uthenticity

☐ **B**ody

☐ **C**reative Energy

☐ **H**eart

☐ **I**dentity

☐ **L**oss and Grief

☐ **R**elationship

Resources, Useful Ideas, Questions, Reflections/Insights, and Symbols Related to:

Chapter 8: Who Have I Been?

GOLDEN NUGGETS:

USEFUL IDEAS:

MY QUESTIONS:

REFLECTIONS/INSIGHTS:

SYMBOL(S):

Chapter 9: Who Am I Now?

GOLDEN NUGGETS:

USEFUL IDEAS:

MY QUESTIONS:

REFLECTIONS/INSIGHTS:

SYMBOL(S):

Chapter 10: Who Am I *Really*?

GOLDEN NUGGETS:

USEFUL IDEAS:

MY QUESTIONS:

REFLECTIONS/INSIGHTS:

SYMBOL(S):

Chapter 11: Five Brief Exercises

GOLDEN NUGGETS:

USEFUL IDEAS:

MY QUESTIONS:

REFLECTIONS/INSIGHTS:

SYMBOL(S):

My Followup List

"Where Am I?" Exercise

Chapter Eight: My Next Step for "Exploring Who I Have Been"

Chapter Nine: My Next Step for "Living in My Midlife Skin"

Chapter Ten: My Next Step for My Direction in Life

"Holes and Empty Places" I Want to Heal

Chapter Eight: Who Have I Been?

Chapter Nine: Who Am I Now?

Chapter Ten: Who Am I Really?

Chapter Eleven: Five Brief Exercises (# 4: Repairs and Mendings)

"Ten Below" Items I Want to Explore Further

Chapter Eight: Who Have I Been?
Item #

Item #

Item #

Chapter Nine: Who Am I Now?
Item #

Item #

Item #

Chapter Ten: <u>Who Am I Really?</u>
Item #

Item #

Item #

Shadow Elements I Want to Make Friends With

Wonderings

What I Want to Let Go of or Leave Behind

What I Want to Begin or Do More Of

Chapter Twelve: Climb Back Up in Your Tree

Glossary Words to Explore Further

Other Notes

Made in the USA
San Bernardino, CA
16 June 2019